NTSB/RAR-10/02
PB2010-916302
Notation 8133C
Adopted July 27, 2010

Railroad Accident Report

Collision of Two Washington Metropolitan Area Transit
Authority Metrorail Trains Near Fort Totten Station
Washington, D.C.
June 22, 2009

**National
Transportation
Safety Board**

490 L'Enfant Plaza, S.W.
Washington, D.C. 20594

National Transportation Safety Board. 2010. *Collision of Two Washington Metropolitan Area Transit Authority Metrorail Trains Near Fort Totten Station, Washington, D.C., June 22, 2009.* **Railroad Accident Report NTSB/RAR-10/02. Washington, DC.**

Abstract: On Monday, June 22, 2009, about 4:58 p.m., eastern daylight time, inbound Washington Metropolitan Area Transit Authority Metrorail train 112 struck the rear of stopped inbound Metrorail train 214. The accident occurred on aboveground track on the Metrorail Red Line near the Fort Totten station in Washington, D.C. The lead car of train 112 struck the rear car of train 214, causing the rear car of train 214 to telescope into the lead car of train 112, resulting in a loss of occupant survival space in the lead car of about 63 feet (about 84 percent of its total length). Nine people aboard train 112, including the train operator, were killed. Emergency response agencies reported transporting 52 people to local hospitals. Damage to train equipment was estimated to be $12 million.

As a result of its investigation of this accident, the National Transportation Safety Board makes recommendations to the U.S. Department of Transportation, the Federal Transit Administration, the Tri-State Oversight Committee, the Board of Directors of the Washington Metropolitan Area Transit Authority, the Washington Metropolitan Area Transit Authority, Alstom Signaling Inc., and six transit systems that use General Railway Signal Company track circuit modules (Massachusetts Bay Transportation Authority, Southeastern Pennsylvania Transportation Authority, Greater Cleveland Regional Transit Authority, Metropolitan Atlanta Regional Transportation Authority, Los Angeles County Metropolitan Transportation Authority, and Chicago Transit Authority).

Contents

Figures

Acronyms and Abbreviations

AIM	Advanced Information Management
Alstom	Alstom Signaling Inc.
APTA	American Public Transportation Association
ARB	always-reporting block (a track circuit indicating that it is occupied when no train is present)
ATC	automatic train control
ATO	automatic train operation
ATP	automatic train protection
ATS	automatic train supervision
BTS	Bureau of Transportation Statistics
C3RS	Confidential Close Call Reporting System
CAMI	Civil Aeromedical Institute
CAP	corrective action plan
cell	cellular
CFR	Code of Federal Regulations
CIT	construction, inspection, and testing
CTA	Chicago Transit Authority
DAM	data acquisition module
D.C. Police	District of Columbia Metropolitan Police Department

DOT	U.S. Department of Transportation
FRA	Federal Railroad Administration
FTA	Federal Transit Administration
GRS	General Railway Signal Company (The company, since acquired by Alstom Signaling Inc., provided the original Metrorail train control modules.)
HRO	high-reliability organization
HVAC	heating, ventilating, and air conditioning
LCD	liquid-crystal display
Metro Police	Metro Transit Police Department
MOC	maintenance operations center
MOU	memorandum of understanding
MSRPH	Metrorail Safety Rules and Procedures Handbook
NRB	non-reporting block (a track circuit indicating that it is vacant although a train is present)
NTSB	National Transportation Safety Board
OCC	Metrorail operations control center
OEM	original equipment manufacturer
Ops.	Operations
PMI	preventive maintenance instruction
RMS	root mean square
TOC	Tri-State Oversight Committee

TSSM   Track Structures System Maintenance

TWC   train-wayside communication

US&S   Union Switch & Signal (The company, now known as Ansaldo STS USA, supplies the components that have begun to replace the GRS equipment originally installed on the Metrorail system.)

VMS   vehicle monitoring system

WMATA   Washington Metropolitan Area Transit Authority

Woodley Park-Zoo/Adams Morgan   Woodley Park

WSAD   warning strobe and alarm device

Executive Summary

On Monday, June 22, 2009, about 4:58 p.m., eastern daylight time, inbound Washington Metropolitan Area Transit Authority (WMATA) Metrorail train 112 struck the rear of stopped inbound Metrorail train 214. The accident occurred on aboveground track on the Metrorail Red Line near the Fort Totten station in Washington, D.C. The lead car of train 112 struck the rear car of train 214, causing the rear car of train 214 to telescope into the lead car of train 112, resulting in a loss of occupant survival space in the lead car of about 63 feet (about 84 percent of its total length). Nine people aboard train 112, including the train operator, were killed. Emergency response agencies reported transporting 52 people to local hospitals. Damage to train equipment was estimated to be $12 million.

Investigation Synopsis

The National Transportation Safety Board's investigation found that the Metrorail automatic train control system stopped detecting the presence of train 214 (the struck train), which caused train 214 to stop and also allowed speed commands to be transmitted to train 112 (the striking train) until the collision. This loss of detection occurred because parasitic oscillation in the General Railway Signal Company (GRS)/Alstom Signaling Inc. (Alstom) track circuit modules was creating a spurious signal that mimicked a valid track circuit signal, thus causing the track circuit to fail to detect the presence of train 214. The investigation found that the track circuit modules did not function safely as part of a fail-safe train control system because GRS/Alstom did not provide a maintenance plan that would detect anomalies in the track circuit signal, such as parasitic oscillation, over the modules' service life and prevent these anomalies from being interpreted as valid track circuit signals.

The investigation examined two near-collisions in 2005 near the Rosslyn Metrorail station that were the result of a loss of train detection. The track circuit in that case failed to detect the presence of stopped trains between the Foggy Bottom and Rosslyn stations. Tests on the circuit modules from the Rosslyn event conducted in 2009 as part of the Fort Totten investigation showed that the Rosslyn modules exhibited parasitic oscillation, and archived data showed that the Rosslyn track circuit had experienced this problem from as far back as 1988 (the earliest time from which data were available). In response to the Rosslyn event, WMATA developed, and issued technical bulletins requiring the use of an enhanced circuit verification test procedure. However, none of the WMATA technicians interviewed as part of this investigation was familiar with the enhanced procedure.

This report explains that WMATA failed to institutionalize and employ systemwide the enhanced track circuit verification test procedure that was developed following the 2005 Rosslyn near-collisions. If the enhanced circuit verification test procedure had been used after recent track circuit work near the Fort Totten accident location, work crews would have been able to determine that the track circuit was failing to detect trains, and actions could have been taken to resolve the problem and prevent the accident.

The report also discusses how shortcomings in WMATA's internal communications, its recognition of hazards, its assessment of risk from those hazards, and its implementation of corrective actions are all evidence of an ineffective safety culture within the organization. Examples described in the report include the low priority that WMATA Metrorail managers placed on addressing malfunctions in the train control system before the accident, which likely influenced the inadequate response to such malfunctions by automatic train control technicians, operations control center controllers, and train operators; and the fact that before the accident the position of chief safety officer lacked the necessary resources and authority, within the organizational structure of WMATA, to adequately identify and address system safety issues and ensure the distribution of safety-critical information throughout the organization.

The report explains the role played in the accident by inadequate or deficient oversight by the Tri-State Oversight Committee and the WMATA Board of Directors and the lack of oversight authority by the Federal Transit Administration. Specifically, the report points out that TOC was ineffective in providing proper safety oversight of WMATA and that the WMATA Board of Directors did not seek adequate information about, nor did it demonstrate adequate oversight to address, the number of open corrective action plans from previous Tri-State Oversight Committee and Federal Transit Administration safety audits of WMATA. The report also explains how the structure of the Federal Transit Administration's current oversight process leads to inconsistent practices, inadequate standards, and marginal effectiveness with respect to state safety oversight of rail transit systems.

With regard to the survivability of the accident, the investigation found that the structural design of the 1000-series railcars offers little occupant protection against a catastrophic loss of survival space in a collision and this contributed to the severity of the occupant injuries and fatalities. In 2006, the National Transportation Safety Board recommended that WMATA accelerate retirement of the 1000-series cars or retrofit them with crashworthiness collision protection comparable to the 6000-series cars. In 2007, that recommendation was classified "Closed—Unacceptable Action" based on WMATA's response that it was not feasible to retrofit the 1000-series cars and that they would remain in service until replacement with the 7000-series cars in 2014.

Probable Cause

The National Transportation Safety Board determines that the probable cause of the June 22, 2009, collision of Washington Metropolitan Area Transit Authority (WMATA) Metrorail train 112 with the rear of standing train 214 near the Fort Totten station was (1) a failure of the track circuit modules, built by GRS/Alstom Signaling Inc., that caused the automatic train control system to lose detection of train 214 (the struck train) and thus transmit speed commands to train 112 (the striking train) up to the point of impact, and (2) WMATA's failure to ensure that the enhanced track circuit verification test (developed following the 2005

Rosslyn near-collisions) was institutionalized and used systemwide, which would have identified the faulty track circuit before the accident.

Contributing to the accident were (1) WMATA's lack of a safety culture, (2) WMATA's failure to effectively maintain and monitor the performance of its automatic train control system, (3) GRS/Alstom Signaling Inc.'s failure to provide a maintenance plan to detect spurious signals that could cause its track circuit modules to malfunction, (4) ineffective safety oversight by the WMATA Board of Directors, (5) the Tri-State Oversight Committee's ineffective oversight and lack of safety oversight authority, and (6) the Federal Transit Administration's lack of statutory authority to provide federal safety oversight.

Contributing to the severity of passenger injuries and the number of fatalities was WMATA's failure to replace or retrofit the 1000-series railcars after these cars were shown in a previous accident to exhibit poor crashworthiness.

Recommendations

The National Transportation Safety Board makes safety recommendations to the U.S. Department of Transportation, the Federal Transit Administration, the Tri-State Oversight Committee, the Washington Metropolitan Area Transit Authority, the Board of Directors of the Washington Metropolitan Area Transit Authority, Alstom Signaling Inc., and six transit systems that use GRS track circuit modules (the Massachusetts Bay Transportation Authority, the Southeastern Pennsylvania Transportation Authority, the Greater Cleveland Regional Transit Authority, the Metropolitan Atlanta Regional Transportation Authority, the Los Angeles County Metropolitan Transportation Authority, and the Chicago Transit Authority).

Factual Information

Accident Synopsis

On Monday, June 22, 2009, about 4:58 p.m., eastern daylight time,[1] inbound Washington Metropolitan Area Transit Authority (WMATA[2]) Metrorail train 112 struck the rear of stopped inbound Metrorail train 214. The accident occurred on aboveground track on the Metrorail Red Line near the Fort Totten station in Washington, D.C. The lead car of train 112 struck the rear car of train 214, causing the rear car of train 214 to telescope[3] into the lead car of train 112, resulting in a loss of occupant survival space in the lead car of about 63 feet (about 84 percent of its total length). (See figure 1.) Nine people aboard train 112, including the train operator, were killed. Emergency response agencies reported transporting 52 people to local hospitals. Damage to train equipment was estimated to be $12 million.

Figure 1. Lead car of striking train (train 112) has overridden last car of struck train (train 214), which has telescoped into lead car of train 112.

---

[1] Unless otherwise noted, all times in this report are eastern daylight time.

[2] Pronounced WAH-MAHT-AH.

[3] *Telescoping* occurs when a railcar body breaches the end structure of another carbody and passes into the structure of that carbody.

Accident Narrative

On the day of the accident, the operator of train 214 (the struck train) reported for the second part of his tour of duty for the day at the Shady Grove station at 3:28 p.m.[4] His first afternoon assignment was to operate Red Line train 214 from Shady Grove to Silver Spring. (See figure 2.) At the time of the accident, he was on his second trip of the afternoon, which consisted of operating Red Line train 214, with six cars, from Silver Spring to Grosvenor-Strathmore.

Figure 2. Schematic of WMATA Metrorail system.

---

[4] Both of the train operators involved in this accident worked some variation of split shifts. The operator of train 214 operated trains during the morning and afternoon rush periods and was off during the middle of the day. Duty times varied for the operator of train 112.

The operator of train 112 (the striking train) reported for duty at Brentwood Yard at 3:50 p.m. Her first assignment was to operate Red Line train 112, also with six cars, from Silver Spring to Shady Grove. She was to depart Silver Spring at 4:33 p.m., following train 214 on inbound track B2.[5]

The operator of train 214 said that he was operating his train in manual mode[6] when he departed Glenmont and that his trip was uneventful until after he departed the Takoma station en route to the next station stop at Fort Totten. Because of an earlier equipment problem with one of the inbound Red Line trains, train traffic was congested, and train 214 was following closely behind train 110. The operator said that he had been slowing his train multiple times because of the presence of train 110. He said that as his train traveled between the Takoma and Fort Totten stations, it "lost speed commands" (meaning that the readouts on the operator's console showed an authorized speed of 0 mph), which caused the train to stop.[7] The operator said that he attributed the loss of speed commands to the proximity of his train to train 110, which was at the Fort Totten station platform at the time. The operator said he expected the speed commands to return momentarily (as soon as train 110 moved out of the station).

Meanwhile, train 112, being operated in automatic mode, was traveling behind train 214. A passenger on train 112 recalled that after leaving the Takoma station, the train stopped, and the operator announced over the train's public address system that another train (which was train 214) was ahead and that they would be moving shortly. The passenger said that the train stopped only briefly, after which it began to move forward and to accelerate to what the passenger estimated was "top speed." Maximum speed for that track segment was 55 mph. (According to recorded train control system data, the speed commands that should have been transmitted to train 112 dropped from 55 mph to 0 mph at 4:56:41. About 39 seconds later, at 4:57:20, speed commands resumed at 55 mph.)

The operator of train 214 said that, after being stopped for what he described as a short time, he felt a "big push" and heard noise toward the rear of his train. He said he noticed that his operator's console had lost power. Recorded data indicate that third-rail power was lost at 4:58:08. (The 750-volt third rail provides power to the trains.) The operator said he looked out the cab window on the right side and saw a train "kind of like on top" and thought a CSX freight train from an adjacent track was involved. The operator thought that the public address system

---

[5] The track in the accident area was designated B1 (for outbound traffic traveling north and away from Metro Center in downtown Washington, D.C.) and B2 (for inbound traffic traveling south toward Metro Center). Although generally considered "inbound" and "outbound," the two main tracks were capable of accommodating trains operating in either direction.

[6] Metrorail trains can be operated in *manual mode*, in which the train operator controls acceleration, braking, and train speed (within limits) or in *automatic mode*, in which all train movements are controlled by the automatic train control (ATC) system while the operator monitors operations.

[7] The Metrorail ATC system (discussed in detail elsewhere in this report) was designed to detect the presence of trains along the main line and to prevent collisions by transmitting speed commands that either stop or slow following trains in order to maintain safe separation. A constant speed command of 0 mph will cause a train operating in either automatic or manual mode to stop. Trains operating in manual mode level 1 (as was train 214) can proceed without speed commands with permission of the Metrorail operations control center (OCC), but they will be limited by the train control system to a maximum speed of 14 mph.

on the train was inoperable because the console did not have power.[8] He said he locked the operator's console and left the operating compartment while carrying his radio.

The train 214 operator said that as he walked through the cars toward the rear of the train, he saw a number of passengers who had been knocked from their seats by the impact. He said he tried to use his portable radio and cellular (cell) phone to contact the Metrorail OCC, but the attempt was unsuccessful. (It was later determined that OCC personnel could hear the operator, but the operator was unable to hear their responses.)

The operator said that when he reached the fourth or fifth car in his train, he encountered smoke. After asking the passengers to move forward on the train, he used the emergency release lever in the car to open a side door, from which he jumped to the ground. Once on the ground and among injured passengers alongside the trains, he successfully established communications with the OCC and reported the collision. He also asked that electrical power to the third rail be cut because of passengers on the ground in the area. He requested emergency medical assistance and then reboarded the train to help injured and trapped passengers.

Moments after the collision, a Red Line controller in the OCC saw on his display screen that the third rail for track B2 (the inbound track) had deenergized (as a result of the collision) in the area of the Takoma and Fort Totten stations. A graphical representation of train 112 was showing on the OCC controller's display screen as occupying track 2 in that area, so he attempted to contact the train operator, but he got no response. About that time, the controller said he heard the operator of train 214 on the radio reporting a collision at chain marker 311+00[9] (about 2,900 feet north of the Fort Totten station).

A Metrorail car equipment maintenance employee was at the Fort Totten station at the time of the accident. The OCC controller sent this employee to the accident area to verify information the OCC was receiving. The OCC also ordered that other trains in the area be held at stations. Train 114 was held at the Takoma station, train 116 was held at the Silver Spring station, and train 110 was held at the Fort Totten station. At 5:10 p.m., the OCC deenergized third-rail power on the adjacent track, B1 (the outbound track).

The operator of train 112 was found fatally injured in the train control compartment. The emergency brake button, or "mushroom," was found in the depressed position. She did not appear to have attempted to leave the control compartment before the collision, and a review of recordings of radio transmissions showed that she had not made a radio call in the moments leading up to the accident.

---

[8] The public address system will work with battery power if the components are not damaged.

[9] *Chain markers* are located at 100-foot intervals along Metrorail rights-of-way. The markers show the line, the track number, and the distance in feet (using surveyors' notation) from that marker to the center of the passenger platform at the Metro Center station. Chain marker 311+00 indicates a distance of 31,100 feet from Metro Center. Measuring between marker posts gives even more precise measurements and more specific locations (such as, for example, chain marker 311+21.3, which is a point 31,121.3 feet from Metro Center that was identified as the point of collision in this accident).

Emergency Response

Initial Notification

Passengers on the accident trains placed the first two 911 calls. The first caller reported a crash on Metrorail at 5:03 p.m. This call was transferred to the Metro Transit Police Department (Metro Police). The second caller reported a train derailment between Takoma and Fort Totten. Another call came from a passenger in the lead car of the striking train. He told investigators he had been sitting in a center-facing seat and estimated that about 15 people were in the car. He said that as the car in which he was riding struck the stopped train, he saw the forward seats and floor coming toward him. He said that when the cars came to rest, he was on top of some seats about 2 feet from the car ceiling. He also said, "both rear side doors were blocked and jammed with no way out." He said,

> I tried to open the door to the back of the car and got it to open, but the door in the next car was blocked by a bulkhead that had collapsed ... the survivors that could walk were directed to exit the car through the rear door window.

A caller who was on a nearby street reported an apparent train derailment in which the train looked as though it could collapse. He reported that the accident occurred on the track between the Fort Totten and Takoma stations near New Hampshire Avenue.

Accident Site Access

The WMATA right-of-way lies between two CSX railroad tracks. To access the accident site, emergency responders had to cut openings in the fences on both sides of the right-of-way and cross the CSX tracks. To control the movement of people in and out of the accident area, only one opening was made on each side of the accident site. In the evening, temporary access was established between 2nd Street NE and the accident site. A CSX assistant division manager called the CSX dispatch center at 5:20 p.m. to notify dispatchers of the accident and to have rail traffic suspended on the CSX tracks in the area.

Resources and Command

At 5:04 p.m., a District of Columbia Fire Department alarm dispatched three engine companies, two truck companies, two battalion chiefs, the special operations battalion chief, a rescue squad, an ambulance, a medic unit, an emergency medical services unit, and a safety officer. These resources were directed to respond to the Takoma station. At 5:10 p.m., a second alarm dispatched two engine companies, a truck company, and a battalion chief to the Fort Totten station. Additional resources were then directed to respond to the Fort Totten station and to 2nd Street NE at Nicholson Street NE. The medic unit was the first to arrive at the accident site about 5:10 p.m.

Two response groups were formed to walk the tracks toward the accident site. One group began from the Fort Totten station, and the second group began from the Takoma station. Once the exact location of the accident was determined, additional resources were directed to respond to Nicholson Street NE. A battalion chief went to the OCC to monitor the response from that location. Mutual aid resources were requested from and provided by Montgomery County and Prince George's County in Maryland and from Fairfax County and Arlington County in Virginia.

A command post was established on New Hampshire Avenue NE on a bridge crossing the right-of-way. The assistant chief of operations for the District of Columbia Fire and Emergency Medical Services Department was the incident commander. A battalion chief was in charge of the evacuation of patients from the trains. The deputy chief for special operations was in charge of rescue and extrication operations. A battalion chief was in charge of medical operations. The District of Columbia Metropolitan Police Department (D.C. Police) and the Metro Police had liaisons at the command post.

Rescue and Recovery Operations

The deputy fire chief said that when he arrived at the scene he saw passengers on both sides of the trains. He reported that some passengers had left the trains unassisted and some had to be rescued by responders. He said he believed that a few of the passengers on the tracks had fallen from the first car of the striking train. A few passengers were standing on top of the rear car of the struck train. The deputy chief verified that the third-rail power was down. Firefighters and Metro Police officers had earlier placed warning strobe and alarm devices[10] (WSAD) on the track structure.

The battalion chief in charge of the evacuation said he saw a haze in the area when he arrived at the scene, but he saw no smoke or fire around the trains. He did not see passengers exiting the trains at that time. An engine company deployed a hose line and charged it with water as a precaution. The battalion chief reported that no rail traffic passed through the area after his arrival. He said that two CSX representatives arrived at the accident site within an hour.

The battalion chief coordinated with a lieutenant from the Metro Police and an assistant chief of the D.C. Police. Metro Police officers established an inner security perimeter around the tracks. The D.C. Police officers established an outer perimeter that included the surrounding neighborhood streets. Transit police officers and firefighters were stationed along the tracks on each side of the accident area to flag and stop any railroad traffic. An accountability system was established to track responders coming into the accident area.

The battalion chief asked police officers to keep the injured passengers on the trains so that firefighters could complete an initial triage of the injured. Some passengers who were able to walk began to evacuate the trains, and firefighters and police officers escorted those passengers to an area established for treating the injured.

---

[10] A *WSAD* is an alerting device that is attached to the third rail when power is down. The WSAD provides a visual and audible alarm if third-rail power is restored.

A number of passengers were trapped in the first car of the striking train when the first firefighters arrived. To access the passengers in the rear of the car, firefighters used saws to cut an opening in the rear side doors. According to the deputy chief, firefighters were able to extricate some passengers quickly after using hydraulic spreaders to enlarge the opening. In the crushed areas of the car, the seats, flooring, and other car structures were compacted, and firefighters first had to remove these components to reach the injured. During this time, additional fire companies were assigned to stabilize the carbody.

Two truck companies were assigned to search the remaining cars. Throughout the response, flexible search cameras and audio equipment were used to monitor the damaged areas of the trains. Firefighting teams with specially trained dogs searched the area surrounding the accident site. Secondary searches were conducted in, under, and around the trains, with no additional survivors found. The deputy chief estimated that about 1.5 hours into the response, all survivors had been rescued.

According to the deputy chief, to continue with safe recovery operations, additional heavy equipment was needed to remove the upper portion of the lead car of the striking train. About 4:00 a.m. on June 23, a crane provided by WMATA arrived at the accident site. The top of the car was lifted from the remainder of the car, and recovery operations continued. The bodies of the last five victims were recovered about 9:00 a.m. on June 23.

Medical Operations

A battalion chief was in charge of the medical branch and treatment area. The treatment area was established to the west of the right-of-way. One of the fire department's mass casualty groups responded.

The battalion chief estimated that about 90 patients were triaged and treated at the treatment area. He estimated that 20 to 25 passengers with minor injuries did not want to be taken to hospitals. Metro Police officers transported these passengers to other Metrorail stations. An ambulance bus transported about 24 passengers to the George Washington University Hospital. The remaining group of about 25 passengers and the operator of train 214 were transported by ambulances. A U.S. National Park Service helicopter transported a patient to Washington Hospital Center. The battalion chief estimated that all patients were treated and transported in about 90 minutes.

Injuries

According to the fire department, 52 patients were transported to hospitals. Two patients had critical injuries; 12 patients were identified as having moderate injuries; the remaining patients had minor injuries. Eight passengers in the lead car of train 112 and the operator of train 112 were killed. According to documents provided by the District of Columbia Office of the Chief Medical Examiner, the fatal injuries were caused by crushing or blunt force trauma.

Damage

The accident occurred on a segment of curved track and resulted in the derailment of the first car and the lead axle of the second car of the striking train. The lead car also sustained catastrophic carbody intrusion damage (telescoping) and loss of occupant survival space to a distance of about 63 feet (about 84 percent of its total length). The rear car of the struck train did not sustain extensive damage and did not derail. None of the other cars on the two trains derailed or sustained major damage. Damage to the train equipment was estimated to be $12 million.

As a result of the derailment, about 20 feet of track was slightly damaged.[11] WMATA estimated about $5,000 in track and appurtenance damage.

Personnel Information

Train 112 Operator

WMATA records showed that the operator of the striking train was hired initially as a bus operator on January 22, 2007. On December 8, 2008, she was reclassified as a train operator, the position she occupied at the time of the accident. She began her rail training on December 8, 2008, and successfully completed the training program on February 11, 2009. WMATA files disclosed no disciplinary action as a train operator prior to the accident.

Time sheets provided by WMATA disclosed the following information for the operator during the 7 days before the accident: On Monday, June 15, she reported for duty at 3:40 p.m. and went off duty at 5:34 p.m. She did not work Tuesday, June 16, and Wednesday, June 17. On Thursday, June 18, she reported for duty at 3:50 p.m. and went off duty at 5:34 p.m. She returned to duty at 6:09 p.m. and worked until 8:14 p.m. She resumed working at 8:38 p.m. and went off duty at 12:59 a.m. the following day, Friday, June 19. She reported for duty later that day at 5:15 p.m. and worked until 11:06 p.m. She resumed working at 11:36 p.m. and went off duty at 4:00 a.m. the following day, Saturday, June 20. She reported for duty that evening at 6:59 p.m. and worked until 10:51 p.m. She resumed working at 11:21 p.m. and went off duty at 3:49 a.m. the following day, Sunday, June 21. She reported for duty later that day at 3:41 p.m. and went off duty the following day, Monday, June 22, at 12:49 a.m. She reported for duty later that day (the day of the accident) at 3:50 p.m. At the time of the accident she had been on duty for 1 hour 10 minutes.

A Metrorail supervisor, who said he had known the operator for between 1 and 1 1/2 months before the accident, recalled that about 4:30 p.m. on the day of the accident he spoke to her by radio. He said he also observed her through an office window at the Glenmont station while she was on her train. The two shared the same off days (Tuesday and Wednesday), and he said they had spoken about looking forward to the time off after working that day. The supervisor said that before the operator departed the station, he saw no evidence that she was

---

[11] Nine crossties were damaged and a section of the third-rail cover was damaged.

tired or fatigued. He said he was not aware of anything that may have preoccupied or distracted her from performing her duties on the day of the accident.

When asked if the operator owned a cell phone, the supervisor said he did not know but that he had never seen her with one. Examination of the operator's cell phone records revealed that between 12:37:37 a.m. and 4:14:58 p.m. on the day of the accident, 11 voice calls were made from her cell phone, and 9 were received. The last activity was an 80-second outgoing call made at 4:14:58 p.m., about 18 minutes before departure from the Glenmont station and 45 minutes before the collision. The records also revealed that on the day of the accident, her cell phone received one text message at 2:27:16 p.m. The records showed no cell phone activity during the time the operator was responsible for operating the train on the day of the accident.

Train 214 Operator

WMATA records indicated that the operator of the struck train was hired initially as a bus driver on February 17, 2000. On October 26, 2001, he was reclassified as a train operator, the position he occupied at the time of the accident.

Efficiency test records showed that the operator of train 214 had received three reprimands and two suspensions since 2003. The first two reprimands occurred in February 2003, one for causing a 6-minute delay and the other for failing to report a station overrun. He had received his third reprimand 1 month before the accident, on May 22, 2009, for failing to take his key before securing a car. He had been suspended in 2004 for passing a red signal on the main track and in 2006 for making an improper coupling that caused equipment damage.

This operator also was removed from service on three occasions in August 2008 for manually stopping his 6-car train at the 8-car marker (the end of the platform) at passenger stations. The operator said he had changed from automatic to manual mode when entering the stations because he did not want to rely on the automated system to properly position the train along the platform.

On the day of the accident, WMATA required that all revenue trains be operated in automatic mode during the morning and evening rush periods. *Metrorail Safety Rules and Procedures Handbook* (MSRPH) Rule 3.20 states that "Mode 1 [automatic train operation] shall be used when carrying revenue passengers except as authorized by OCC or as specified in the current General Order." No modifications to MSRPH Rule 3.20 were in effect at the time of the accident. After the accident, WMATA directed that all trains were to be operated in manual mode for an indefinite period until the integrity and reliability of the ATC system could be assured. Further, all trains would be required to pull forward to the 8-car marker when making station stops.

The operator had been sent for reinstruction on manual door opening as well as for retraining on coupling and uncoupling procedures; main line operations utilizing stopping profiles; and troubleshooting and procedures on doors, brakes, circuit breakers, and location. He also was retrained on train recovery procedures and blocking/clamping operation procedures. WMATA managers stated that action was taken because the operator was not maintaining his train's schedule while operating in manual mode and as a consequence was delaying trains. Contrary to instructions to return to automatic mode, the operator continued to operate his train manually. He stated that he was permitted to take this action under MSRPH Rule 3.1, which states the following:

> Passenger safety is the responsibility of every WMATA employee; however, the Train Operators have the ultimate and final responsibility for the safety of the passengers on their particular trains.

Time sheets from WMATA disclosed that the operator had worked essentially the same schedule on each of his 5 work days before the accident: beginning work at 6:44 a.m. and working until 10:19 a.m., then returning to work at 3:18 p.m. and going off duty at 6:46 p.m. He worked Monday through Friday and was off Saturday and Sunday. On Monday, June 22, he reported for duty as usual at 6:44 a.m. and went off duty at 10:19 a.m. He returned to work at 3:18 p.m. At the time of the accident he had been on duty for about 1 hour 40 minutes.

A Metrorail supervisor who said he had known the operator for between 4 and 5 years said that he spoke with the operator for 3 or 4 minutes about 4:00 p.m. on the day of the accident. He said that he did not notice anything unusual about the operator and that he did not exhibit any indications of being fatigued. He also said that the operator did not appear to be distracted or under the influence of alcohol or drugs.

Medical and Toxicological Information

After the accident, WMATA made arrangements to have three OCC employees who were on duty at the time of this accident—an assistant superintendent, an OCC supervisor, and a Red Line controller—undergo postaccident toxicological testing. Testing was conducted between 8:17 p.m. and 9:10 p.m. on the day of the accident for ethyl alcohol (based on breath specimens) and for illegal drugs (based on urine specimens), including marijuana metabolites, cocaine metabolites, opiates, amphetamines, and phencyclidine. The results for all tested employees were negative for the presence of alcohol and those drugs.

Specimens of blood, serum, and urine were obtained at the Washington Hospital Center from the operator of train 214. Medical records showed that on the day of the accident a blood specimen from the operator was received at the hospital laboratory at 9:11 p.m. and a urine specimen at 8:52 p.m. The specimens were also sent to the Civil Aeromedical Institute (CAMI) in Oklahoma City, Oklahoma, for independent toxicological analysis. CAMI tested for the presence of ethanol (alcohol) and amphetamines, opiates, marijuana, cocaine, phencyclidine, benzodiazepines, barbiturates, antidepressants, antihistamines, meprobamate, methaqualone, and nicotine. The results were negative for alcohol and drugs. In addition, the Washington Hospital Center performed toxicological testing for alcohol based on a blood sample. A urine sample was tested for barbiturates, cocaine, marijuana, opiates, phencyclidine, amphetamines, and benzodiapines. All results were negative.

The Federal Transit Administration (FTA), which is the agency responsible for regulating postaccident toxicological testing of transit employees, has no mechanism for obtaining specimens from an employee who has been killed in an accident. The National Transportation Safety Board (NTSB), using its own authority, obtained specimens from the autopsy of the operator of train 112, and these specimens were also sent to CAMI for toxicological analysis. The results were negative for the presence of alcohol and other drugs, including amphetamines, opiates, marijuana, cocaine, phencyclidine, benzodiazepines, barbiturates, antidepressants, antihistamines, meprobamate, methaqualone, and nicotine. Ibuprofen was detected in the blood specimen.

Meteorological Information

The accident occurred during daylight. The weather was reported as dry (no active precipitation). Skies were clear with 10-mile visibility. The wind was at 13 mph, and the temperature was 84° F.

Postaccident Equipment Inspection and Testing

Investigators inspected both trains after the collision. The front portion of the first car of train 112 (the striking train) had overridden and was breached by the last car of train 214. This breaching, or telescoping action, resulted in a "wall" of collision debris that consisted of a tightly compressed mass of dislodged, displaced, and crushed seats, floor and ceiling panels, stanchion posts, and other interior elements. The collision debris extended a linear distance of about 13 feet, and along with the 50 feet of telescoping penetration, resulted in a loss of occupant survival space in the striking car of about 63 feet (about 84 percent of its total length). Some components of this mass of debris spilled out of the car, apparently as a result of the separated carbody sidewall and roof panels. Some of the debris came to rest on the track bed, as did most of the underfloor suspension and propulsion components of the car.

Most of the damage from the collision was sustained by the lead car of train 112. Both cars came to rest upright and substantially aligned with the track. The lead and second cars of the striking train derailed; these were the only cars on either train to do so. The other railcars of each train were wedged together but were otherwise substantially undamaged and did not lose any occupant survival space. No evidence of fire was apparent in any of the railcars, nor was there evidence of release of a hazardous material such as battery acid.

Both the front and rear trucks of the lead car of train 112 separated from the carbody during the collision, but the brakes on the wheels of these trucks, as well as on all the other wheels of both trains, were found to be tightly clamped. No evidence was found of binding, dragging, or fouling of the brake rigging on either train. Inspections of the wheels on train 112 did not detect wheel flats,[12] and no flat spots were visually or audibly[13] evident when the less damaged cars were moved into the shop at Brentwood Yard.

---

[12] *Wheel flat* refers to a wheel that has either developed a flat spot or gone "out of round" as a result of being dragged along the rail head. Wheel flats often result from locked or misapplied brakes.

[13] The sound of a flat spot on a wheel is a repetitive banging as the flat spot hits the rail each time the wheel turns.

The electronic brake control units were removed from the first two cars of the striking train. NTSB investigators were able to download fault log entries for both units, which showed that no faults in the braking system of either car had been recorded within the 2 days leading up to the accident.[14] A test of the brake system on the four trailing cars of the striking train revealed that brake pressure was within design specifications for all levels of brake application and that all the cars met or exceeded brake rate standards.

Polishing and wear patterns on the braking components in every instance were consistent with a fully functioning system. Bluing[15] that was found on the lead car's braking components was consistent with that found on other cars on which new brake pads had recently been installed. Such bluing is typical during the wear-in period for a new pad.

Investigators examined the control compartments on both trains. The control console of train 112 was covered with a layer of broken window glazing and other debris but was generally intact. The emergency brake mushroom was found in the depressed, or *stop*, position. The button operated freely when manually released and depressed, making a distinctive "snapping" sound when operated in either direction. The automatic train operation (ATO) selector was in the "auto" position; the automatic train protection (ATP) switch on the operator's panel (see figure 3) was properly positioned for revenue service and was cut in and sealed,[16] and the master controller was in the "Auto/Store" position. The key was missing from the key-up switch, and the switch was in the "off" position. When another key was inserted, the switch operated.

Postaccident examination of the control compartment of train 214 (the struck train) revealed that the emergency brake mushroom was up, the selection switch was in the "Auto/Store" position, the key-up switch was in the "off" position, and the master controller was in the "Auto/Store" position.

Postaccident Site Inspection

The collision occurred on Metrorail main line track designated B2 that is normally used for inbound (southbound, toward Metro Center) traffic. At the request of the NTSB, the footprint[17] of the collision and derailment was photographed and surveyed by the Federal Bureau of Investigation and surveyed by the WMATA engineering department. Marks were evident on the rail head at chain marker 311+21.3 that appeared to have been caused by a wheel flange as it climbed up and over the rail head and struck rail anchors and crossties. Investigators determined that these marks represented the point of collision and subsequent derailment. The point of collision was thus on track B2 about 2,935 feet north of the Fort Totten station and about

---

[14] The most recent brake faults recorded had occurred on June 20, 2008. The two faults recorded for the lead car were "Brake Stuck 'On'" and "Brake Response Fail." For the second car, the faults recorded were "Slip Timer Expired" and "Brake Response Fail."

[15] *Bluing* refers to a blue oxide film on the polished rotors due to an extremely high temperature (600° F or higher).

[16] The switch was in the "on" position with an unbroken seal.

[17] The *footprint* included all visible evidence, such as marks on the ties, marks on the track components and on the rail, and the positions of involved passenger cars and car components.

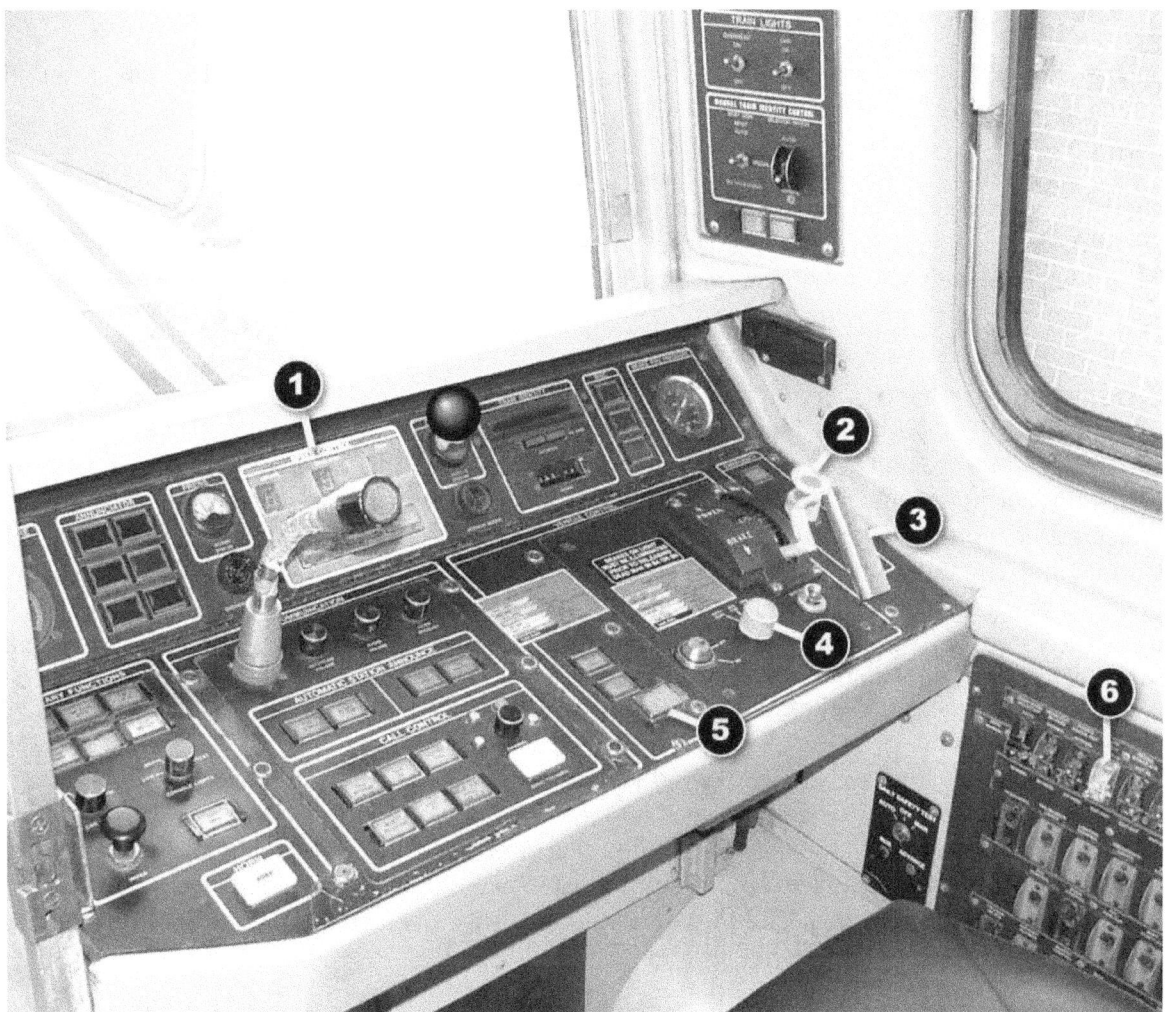

Figure 3. Exemplar Rohr 1000-series car operator's console: (1) speed control indicator panel, (2) emergency brake "mushroom," (3) master control handle, (4) mode director switch, (5) automatic train operation stop, and (6) automatic train protection cutout switch.

6,790 feet south of the Takoma station. Investigators used event recorder data to determine that the struck train moved about 10 feet after impact. This measurement was consistent with the measurements taken at the footprint of the collision.

A postaccident visual track inspection was conducted on track B2 between chain markers 322+00 and 311+00. Nothing remarkable was noted concerning track geometry, including gage (distance between running rails), curve alignment, and superelevation (relative height of the two running rails in a curve) when the measurements were compared with WMATA main line standards. Skid marks were found on both rail head surfaces. The skid marks appeared to have been the result of wheel-to-rail braking friction. No indications of dragging equipment or any other marks on the track were observed during the visual inspection of that area. The rail head appeared to be free of corrugations[18] and other indications of fatigue or wear. No rail or wheel lubricant was apparent on the rail heads.

In addition to the postaccident visual track inspection, track geometry measurements for gage, cross-level, alignment, and rail side wear were conducted between markers 313+00 and 309+00. Again, nothing remarkable was noted during that inspection when the measurements were compared with WMATA main line track standards.

Operations Information

The trackage and railroad equipment involved in this accident are owned and operated by WMATA, an integrated regional passenger transit system organized to provide bus and rail transit service to the National Capital Area, which includes the District of Columbia and several surrounding counties of Virginia and Maryland. Metrorail is the division of WMATA that provides rail transit service. The Metrorail system comprises five operating rail lines identified by color: Red, Blue, Orange, Yellow, and Green.[19] Metrorail began train operations on March 27, 1976, with limited service on the Red Line. The system as originally designed was completed with the opening of the last passenger stations in January 2001.

The Metrorail system is the second largest (by number of passengers) rail transit system in the United States. It owns and operates 86 passenger stations and more than 1,100 passenger cars. The system consists of about 106.3 miles of main line track, which includes tracks that are underground (subway), at grade, or elevated. In fiscal year 2008 (the most recent data available), Metrorail provided more than 222 million passenger trips, averaging about 608,200 passenger trips per day.

Typically, 253 inbound trains and 253 outbound trains traverse the accident area each day Monday through Thursday. On Fridays, 264 inbound trains and 264 outbound trains traverse the area. On Saturdays and Sundays, the trains number 153 trains in each direction. Weekday morning inbound rush-hour[20] is from 5:00 a.m. to 9:30 a.m.; evening outbound rush-hour is from 3:00 p.m. to 7:00 p.m.

---

[18] Rail *corrugations*, sometimes called "washboard rail," are variations in the "smoothness" of the rail head surface that can affect wheel-rail contact.

[19] The five operating rail lines are interconnected and are not separate operations. The Red Line is the only line that does not share at least a part of its route with one of the other operating lines.

[20] The time when peak ridership occurs.

Track Information

General

In the area of the collision are four at-grade railroad tracks. (See figure 4.) Looking northward (toward the Takoma station) the easternmost track is CSX railroad main line track No. 1. The next two adjacent tracks are WMATA tracks B1 (outbound) and B2 (inbound), which was the accident track in this case. The westernmost track is CSX main line track No. 2. The two WMATA tracks are parallel, with a track centerline distance between the two of 14 feet. Fencing separates the WMATA tracks from the CSX tracks, with additional fencing preventing trespasser access to the CSX tracks. The centerline distance between the CSX westernmost track and the WMATA inbound track (B2) is about 20 feet; between the CSX easternmost track and the WMATA outbound track (B1), centerline distance is about 22 feet.

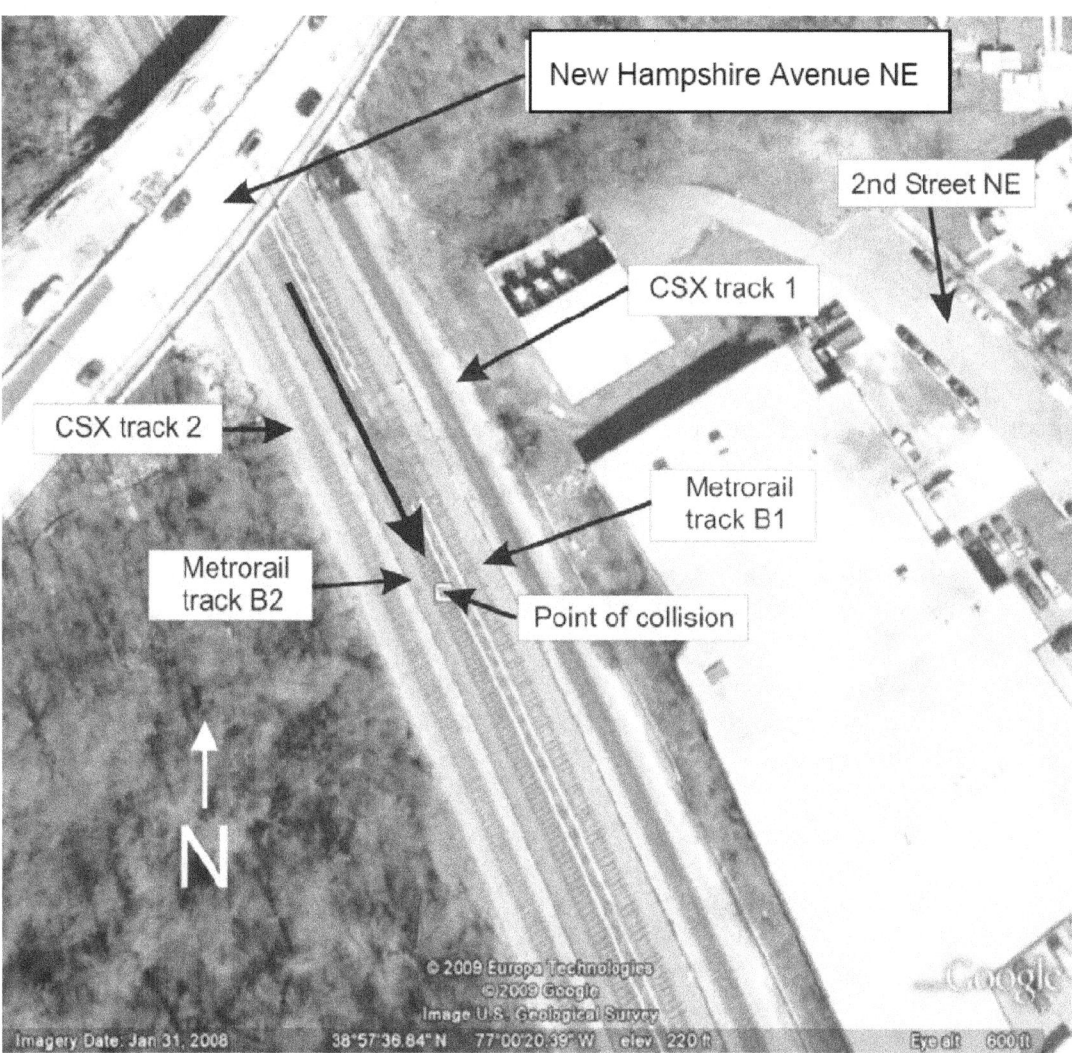

Figure 4. Aerial view of accident site.

Train propulsion power is provided from an electrified third rail.[21] The third rail for inbound trains is to the east of and parallel to track B2. The distance from the center of the third rail to the inside edge of the nearest running rail is 2 feet 2 inches. The third rail is about 4.5 inches higher than the nearest running rail and is shielded by a cover to protect WMATA workers and others from accidental contact.

The collision occurred at chain marker 311+21.3, which is in a curve. The curve begins at chain marker 323+40.84 and ends at chain marker 300+77.65, with the body of the curve between markers 320+91.23 and 303+28.43 (representing 1,762.80 feet). The curve is a 1°15' right hand (in the southbound or inbound direction) curve with a superelevation of 5 inches.

Track B2 is designated to be maintained and inspected in accordance with WMATA main line standards and to be capable of carrying trains at 75 mph even though WMATA has a speed limit of 59 mph on the Red Line. The track in the accident area is 115-pound continuous welded rail[22] affixed with Pandrol spring clip fasteners[23] and with tie plates and 6-inch "cut" track spikes onto wooden crossties. The wooden crossties are spaced about every 27 inches on center. When defective crossties are replaced, Pandrol fasteners are used. Pandrol plates are fastened onto the wooden crossties with lag screws; the other tie plates are fastened with the "hair pin" style of nail/pin fasteners and/or track spikes. Drive-on type rail anchors are applied to the rail to prevent longitudinal rail movement in the older crosstie locations.

Track Inspections

The WMATA Track, Structures, and System Maintenance Division, and specifically the Track Department within that division, is responsible for inspecting and maintaining Metrorail track. According to WMATA representatives, much of the daily activity is centered on twice-weekly walking/visual track inspections. Track inspectors produce reports (Track Walker Inspection Reports) of their inspections, which they then submit for review by their department managers. The reports cover track defects, track maintenance items, and updates on known issues. Specialized automated equipment is also used to conduct additional track geometry inspections and inspections for internal rail defects.

According to WMATA representatives, track maintenance and track defect repairs are based in large part on the track inspectors' reports. Track repairs are documented, and track inspectors verify that the repairs were completed.

---

[21] Paddles extending from the undercarriage of the train ride along the surface of the third rail and conduct power from the third rail to the train's traction motors.

[22] *Continuous welded rail* consists of rail sections that have been welded together in lengths greater than 400 feet.

[23] Pandrol spring clip fasteners are designed to fasten the rail to the tie plates and, when attached to the crosstie, will retard longitudinal rail movement.

Visual Track Inspections. Two track inspectors (working as a team)[24] conduct twice-weekly walking/visual inspections of the Red Line track in the accident area. The last inspection on track B2 before the accident was on June 20, 2009. No track defects were noted on the Track Walker Inspection Report. Investigators also reviewed track inspection reports from January 4, 2009, through June 20, 2009. Nothing remarkable was noted regarding the track in the area of the collision, but one track inspection record for that section of track was missing (for the week of March 22, 2009).

Automated Track Inspections. WMATA contracted for an automated track geometry inspection to be performed four times per year. The most recent inspection through the area of the collision was on April 8, 2009. On January 16, 2009, lateral load testing was conducted in conjunction with the track geometry testing through the area of the collision. Nothing remarkable was noted during this inspection and testing.

On January 17, 2009, the rail head profile was measured by laser. The profile measurement that was nearest the collision area was taken at marker 316+18. Rail head wear was found to be minimal.

The rail on WMATA track structure is ultrasonically inspected by a contractor five times per year. The last inspection before the collision was on March 18, 2009. No rail defects were detected in the area of the collision. On July 23, 2009, as part of a scheduled inspection, the rails of track B2 between Takoma and Fort Totten were ultrasonically inspected for internal rail defects. No defects or discontinuities were noted.

Track Maintenance

The most recent major track maintenance work performed through the area of the accident was a track surfacing operation. Production tamping and ballast regulating were conducted on track B2 between Takoma and Fort Totten on September 28, 2008, according to a Track Production Daily Work Report.

On April 24 and 25, 2009, crossties, Pandrol tie plates, and third-rail insulators were installed on track B2 at the Takoma interlocking.[25] Surfacing and ballast work associated with the new installation were performed on April 26, 2009.

On May 4 and 5, 2009, crossties and Pandrol tie plates were replaced on track B2 at Fort Totten. Then ballast was dumped, and the crossties were tamped with automated hand tools in that area.

---

[24] One person serves as the primary inspector while the second, also a track inspector, serves as the lookout for train traffic.

[25] *Interlockings* are sites at which tracks join together or cross. An interlocking includes the track switches and associated signals and control machinery necessary to connect the track and to ensure safe operation through the connected or crossing track.

Train and Mechanical Information

The Metrorail fleet consists of self-propelled, single-level, two-truck, electrically powered (through the third rail) passenger cars supplied by four manufacturers: Rohr[26] (1000-series cars),[27] Breda[28] (2000, 3000, and 4000 series), CAF[29] (5000 series), and Alstom[30] (6000 series). All cars in the fleet were built to allow for functional and operational compatibility. WMATA is in the process of purchasing new cars (to be designated the 7000-series and tentatively scheduled to enter the inventory starting in 2013) to replace the 1000-series cars, which are the oldest in the Metrorail fleet. At the time of the accident, the Metrorail passenger car fleet consisted of 294 Rohr cars (26 percent of the fleet), 464 Breda cars (41 percent of the fleet), 192 CAF cars (17 percent of the fleet), and 84 Alstom cars (16 percent of the fleet). The service life span of the Rohr cars was not specified in procurement documents. The specified service life spans of the subsequently purchased cars were 30 years for the Breda cars, 35 years for the CAF cars, and 40 years for the Alstom cars.

In general, Metrorail cars are about 75 feet long, about 10 feet wide, and about 11 feet high. The carbody is constructed principally of aluminum alloy extrusions and formed shapes, with welded steel subassembly components used for certain load-bearing elements. The front-end cowl assembly of the cars is molded fiberglass that incorporates a pair of collision post and corner post elements. The exterior skin of the roof, sidewalls, and rear end-panel is aluminum sheet metal.

The train operator occupies a control compartment at one end of the car (the front end), with the passenger compartment occupying the balance of the carbody. Seating in the passenger compartment is generally provided by a series of transverse-mounted, paired seat-set assemblies configured on both sides of a longitudinal center aisle passageway.[31] Numerous hand-hold stanchion posts and handrails are fitted throughout the passenger compartment. Each car has six passenger doors, three on each side, and a single emergency exit door (allowing movement between cars) at each end.

As published in specification and procurement documents, a full passenger load for a Metrorail car is 175, including both seated and standing passengers. "Crush load" (the maximum number of passengers that can possibly be accommodated both seated and standing very close

---

[26] Built by Rohr Industries, which is no longer in business.

[27] Metrorail cars are individually numbered, with the number series identifying the original car manufacturer.

[28] Breda Construzioni Ferroviarie S.p.A of Italy.

[29] Construcciones Y Auxiliar de Ferrocarriles, Madrid, Spain, fabricated the carbody shell, and AAI Transportation Systems, in Hunt Valley, Maryland, provided the final carbody assembly.

[30] Alstom Transport, Saint Ouen Cedex, France, fabricated the carbody shell, and Alstom Transportation, Inc., in Hornell, New York, provided the technical support (that is, the final carbody assembly).

[31] Passenger seating also includes center-facing seat pairs next to passenger doors as priority seating for senior citizens and people with disabilities.

together) is 232.[32] "Absolute maximum load" (based on the load capacity of the carbody floor) is 252.

In revenue service, sequentially numbered pairs of Metrorail cars are semipermanently coupled together and operate only in "married-pair" railcar sets. The railcars are coupled together at the ends opposite the operator's compartment and are thus said to be in a "back-to-back" orientation. The minimum Metrorail train has two cars consisting of a single married-pair car set.[33] The maximum-length train is four married-pair car sets for a total of eight cars. The typical revenue service Metrorail train consists of six cars (three married-pair car sets), with 4- or 8-car trains placed in service as needed.

All six of the cars making up train 112 on the day of the accident were 1000-series cars manufactured by Rohr. On train 214, the four cars in the lead were 3000-series cars manufactured by Breda; they were followed by two 5000-series cars manufactured by CAF.

NTSB investigators reviewed Metrorail equipment inspection and maintenance procedures and practices. Investigators also monitored routine equipment inspections and performed random inspections of train sets in revenue service. The Brentwood Yard car repair facility also was appraised for staff training and knowledge, repair manual currency, preventive maintenance scheduling, and repair techniques. No problems were identified.

Investigators also reviewed inspection and repair records for the cars making up the train 112 consist on the day of the accident. WMATA requires that all 1000-series cars receive a periodic inspection every 30 days. Records indicated that these inspections were current for all cars on the train. The records also revealed that maintenance actions had been deferred on five of the six cars on the train because of a lack of repair parts. Most of the deferred actions involved replacement of brake control valves.

Metrorail Railcar Crashworthiness

Because of concerns about the crashworthiness of the 1000-series cars, after the accident, WMATA began placing the cars in the middle (belly) of trains with cars of a later design on either side. According to WMATA, this "bellying" of the cars was intended to reduce the vulnerability of the cars to catastrophic damage during a collision by providing a "buffer" of more crashworthy cars around them. In testimony at the public hearing on this accident held at NTSB Headquarters on February 23–25, 2010, the WMATA chief vehicle engineer stated that bellying the cars was an operational decision and that no engineering analysis had been done to evaluate its effectiveness in preventing catastrophic damage to the 1000-series cars in the event of a collision.

---

[32] According to WMATA, informal testing and field observations indicate that, in practice and because of the personal belongings most passengers carry, the maximum number of passengers a Metrorail car can accommodate is about 175, seated and standing.

[33] Under current WMATA practices, such 2-car trains are not operated in revenue service.

After the public hearing and in response to an NTSB request, the WMATA chief vehicle engineer performed an analysis to predict the behavior of a 1000-series car in a 15-mph head-on collision with a car of a different series.[34] The analysis was based on the information gleaned from actual low-speed collisions between cars *without* crash energy management[35] design elements (the 1000-series cars) and cars *with* such elements (the later-series cars). The analysis determined that the carbody of the 1000-series cars may fail during a collision at speeds between 11.6 and 14.8 mph. This could be classified as a low-speed collision, with carbody structural failure that would likely initiate behind the front-end underframe assembly at its connection with the sidesill, toward the center of the car in the doorway. The analysis stated that a reasonable assumption would be that a collision at such speeds would not likely result in a serious loss of interior space (from telescoping).

Automatic Train Control Overview

The WMATA Metrorail system operates under an ATC system that was designed to allow for fully automated train operations requiring little direct involvement by train operators. Designed during the original construction of the Metrorail system in the early 1970s, that system, or its primary elements, remains in use today in many locations throughout the system.

ATC Subsystems

The Metrorail ATC system consists of three subsystems:

Automatic Train Protection. The ATP subsystem is a wayside, meaning along the rail, system designed to provide protection against collision and train overspeed through the automatic block signaling system.[36] In addition, the ATP subsystem provides control of interlockings, route security through interlockings, and control of train door operations.

The ATP subsystem maintains train separation by transmitting speed commands to each train based on the instantaneous track occupancy conditions ahead of the train (in the direction of travel) and on the status of any interlockings ahead of the train. The speed commands are generated at a nearby train control room[37] and are sent to the trains via a coded audio frequency

---

[34] *Vehicle Crashworthiness Assessment,* Washington Metropolitan Area Transit Authority Office of the Chief Engineer - Vehicles (Washington, DC: Washington Metropolitan Area Transit Authority, 2010).

[35] Includes features designed to control collision energy to protect the occupied volumes of the railcar from crushing and to limit the decelerations on the occupants in those volumes. See Title 49 *Code of Federal Regulations* (CFR) 238.5, "Definitions," for more information.

[36] The automatic block system is a wayside system that detects the location of trains and selects the proper speed command to be transmitted to the train to ensure that civil speed limits are observed and that safe train separation is maintained.

[37] Most train control rooms are at passenger stations, but some are at other sites along the track wayside.

signal injected into the track whenever a track circuit[38] is indicating that it is occupied.[39] These speed commands are locally generated, are not relayed to the OCC, and cannot be modified by the OCC. The ATC system was designed never to allow trains to exceed the ATP speed command in normal operation.

Automatic Train Supervision. The automatic train supervision (ATS) subsystem is primarily a wayside system with some OCC inputs. The ATS system is designed to control train routing and scheduling. Scheduling is accomplished first by automatic equipment at the wayside, then, second, by computer programs at the OCC, which are automatically triggered when necessary to provide for minor schedule adjustments to maintain traffic flow and scheduling.

A train number and a destination are initially provided to each train by the OCC rail operations computer system. This information is stored on board the train. As the train passes through a passenger station (or passes selected areas along the track), this information is repeated back from the train to the OCC. This information and block occupancy reports are used to track train movements through the rail system and to display those movements on the OCC controllers' display screens. When a train reports arrival at a station, an algorithm in the OCC computer determines if a schedule adjustment is needed. If it is, the ATS subsystem can transmit a new acceleration profile and running speed to the train via track-to-wayside communications. The OCC computer can also alert an OCC controller if required.

Automatic Train Operation. The ATO subsystem is primarily a wayside system. The ATO subsystem is designed to manage train startup and acceleration, maintain running speed en route, and stop the train smoothly at the proper position along the station platform. Running speed is based on the lower of three speeds: the maximum permitted (ATP) speed, the ATS speed, and the programmed station stop speed profile.

The programmed station stop speed profile is generated in the train based on proximity sensors in the track wayside that signal to the train the presence of and distance to an upcoming station platform. As a train approaches a station, ATC data are supplemented with data from a wayside marker system (part of the ATO subsystem). About 2,700 feet from a station platform centerline, as the train passes over passive tuned coils located between the rails, communication is initiated between the train and a wayside ATO marker coil. Based on the tuned frequency of the marker, the train's ATO logic initiates a station stop. As the train continues to approach the station, it passes over additional passive tuned coils that update the distance remaining and enable trains to slow and stop at a predetermined location along a station platform.

The ATO subsystem is also designed to handle dispatching from station platforms. Automatic timers triggered by train arrival hold the train at the station for scheduling

---

[38] Metrorail main line track is divided into electrically discrete *blocks* of track varying in length from 39 feet to 1,565 feet. Each block generally defines a *track circuit*. In this report, the terms *block* and *track circuit* are used interchangeably.

[39] Thus, if a track circuit is unoccupied, or if the signal system falsely interprets an occupied track circuit as being unoccupied, no speed commands will be transmitted to trains occupying that track circuit, and the ATP and ATS speed readouts on train operators' consoles will revert to 0 mph.

adjustments. These dwell times can be modified from the OCC as needed to adjust for scheduling changes.

Speed Commands

The electronic and electrical components necessary to implement the ATP, ATS, and ATO subsystems are mounted on racks in train control rooms located at each Metrorail passenger station. (See figure 5.) Each train control room contains the electronics associated with the track circuits monitored and controlled from that location.

Figure 5. Racks of automatic train control components at Fort Totten train control room.

Speed commands sent by the ATC system are displayed on train operators' consoles. Each operator console displays three speed readouts. The first readout is the ATP speed (labeled and sometimes referred to as the "limiting" speed and representing the maximum speed the ATP subsystem will allow a train to attain over that route segment). The second readout is the ATS speed (labeled and sometimes referred to as the "regulated" speed and representing the maximum speed authorized by the rail operations computer system). The third readout, labeled "train" speed, displays the train's actual speed.

If the ATC system determines that a train should stop to provide safe separation from another train, the ATP speed transmitted to that train will be 0 mph. By design, if a train does not receive speed commands for any reason, the ATP and ATS speeds will default to 0 mph as a fail-safe[40] measure.

Train Operating Modes

The degree of automation under which Metrorail trains operate is partially determined through the use of the following three operating modes:

Mode 1 (automatic). Normal train functions, including acceleration, speed, and braking, are controlled by the ATC system, with the operator responsible for monitoring console indicators and track conditions. The striking train was operating in this mode at the time of the accident and, according to Metrorail representatives, all trains in revenue service at the time of the accident were expected to be operated in mode 1.

Mode 2, Level 1 (manual with speed protection). Train acceleration and braking are manually controlled by the train operator, with overspeed protection provided by the ATP subsystem. The struck train was operating in this mode at the time of the accident. Although, according to WMATA, the operator should have been operating in mode 1, he said he chose to operate in mode 2 because he preferred to stop at the platform marker for 8-car trains rather than the marker for 6-car trains (which the ATO subsystem would have enforced) to ensure that his train was safely inside the station before the doors opened regardless of the number of cars in the train. (Since the accident, all Metrorail trains are operated in mode 2, with the 8-car marker being the uniform stopping position.)

Mode 3 (manual with ATP cutout). All train operations are controlled by the operator, with no overspeed protection. This operating mode is only used when malfunctioning equipment makes mode 1 or 2 operation impossible.

Monitoring and Control of Train Operations

Train operations on the Metrorail system are carried out under the authority and supervision of the Metrorail operations control center (referred to in this report as the OCC), located in downtown Washington, D.C. The OCC is responsible for providing positive control over all station activities, train movements, and subsystems (power, ATC, automatic fare collection, and communications) necessary for the efficient movement of passengers. The OCC also manages all emergency situations, which includes contacting fire, police, and medical services as required.

---

[40] *Fail-safe* is a design philosophy applied to safety-critical systems. The fail-safe principle requires that a system be prohibited from assuming an unsafe state in the event of a component failure.

The OCC, employing a central computer system supervised by human controllers, implements train control strategies as necessary to regulate traffic flow. These control strategies may be preprogrammed strategies that are carried out automatically by the central control mainframe computer, or they may be strategies implemented manually by OCC line controllers.

One mechanism by which OCC controllers exercise manual control of trains is through the ATS subsystem, which is primarily responsible for train routing and scheduling. For example, controllers can, through the ATS subsystem, modify train running speeds[41] as a way of adjusting train schedules. Such modifications can be relayed to the trains only when the train has established train-wayside communication (TWC) within the limits of a passenger station. Controllers cannot modify speed commands that are transmitted to trains by the wayside ATP system, which are based on instantaneous train occupancy detection.

Between stations, the OCC can manually control train movements by changing signal aspects or switch alignments at interlockings at certain control points or through direct communication with train operators via a two-way radio system. The OCC monitors and controls train movements through three consoles, designated Operations (Ops.) 1, Ops. 2, and Ops. 3. Each console is normally staffed by two controllers—a radio controller[42] and a train controller.[43]

Each control console incorporates an array of liquid-crystal display (LCD) screens that provide a graphic representation of the line segment(s) being monitored. (See figure 6.) At the Ops. 1 and Ops. 2 consoles, three screens on either side of the central console display train and track information to the radio controller on one side and the train controller on the other. A single, shared LCD screen displays alarm information to both controller positions. The console is designed so that the radio- and train-controller positions can be worked from either side of the console. The console can also be worked by one controller in the absence of the other. The Ops. 3 console has four LCD screens on each side and a single shared alarm screen. The alarm display for each control console is programmed to display only those alarms for the portion of the Metrorail system under the authority of that console.

Metrorail line controllers work in three 8-hour shifts. OCC supervisory personnel work similar shifts and typically include an OCC assistant superintendent and an OCC supervisor.

Data Transfer and Communication

Communication between the rail operations computer system and field elements takes place through 96 remote terminal units (90 in train control rooms at passenger stations and 6 at

---

[41] The ATS subsystem can limit the speed commands that can be transmitted to trains at certain locations.

[42] The *radio controller* communicates with train operators by radio and is responsible for ensuring conformance with policies and procedures and for keeping train operators and personnel informed of all unusual occurrences on the railroad. The radio controller also communicates with supervisors and maintenance personnel in the field.

[43] The *train controller* is responsible for such tasks as setting route alignments and signals, setting train performance levels, and coordinating the addition or replacement of trains when necessary.

yards and interlockings) and 23,118 monitored or controlled data "nodes" throughout the Metrorail system.

Figure 6. Line controller console in Metrorail operations control center.

Various sensors and subsystems positioned across the Metrorail system collect data reflecting the status of more than 200 distinct operational parameters such as track circuit occupancies, switch positions, signal aspects, and train-to-wayside communications. In general, these data are first concentrated at a nearby remote terminal unit (1 of the 96 units currently in use). Once per second, the main computer system polls each remote terminal unit. The units respond by immediately returning status data as gathered by the sensors and subsystems.

The remote terminal units on the Metrorail system are electronic data multiplexing systems with varying installation dates; some have been in place as long as 35 years. The original units are hardware-based devices using discrete logic chips; newer designs are generally microprocessor-based. The major manufacturers of remote terminal units in use by WMATA are (oldest to newest): TRW, Ferranti, GRS, and Horton.

The TWC system provides two-way data communication between carborne and wayside train control systems. This system provides for automatic door operation at stations and for carborne passenger information displays. The wayside system transmits signals to the train using track circuit transmitters. These signals are picked up by receiver coils mounted underneath the lead car of a train. A transmit loop mounted under the front of the lead car transmits information about the train to the wayside system.

Data Management and Train Status Display

The software used to manage the data transmitted to the OCC from remote terminal units in the field was developed by Aeronautical Radio, Inc., and is known as the Advanced Information Management (AIM) system. Using AIM data, a graphics package called "Animator" creates the information displayed on OCC controller LCD screens. The AIM display was designed to provide controllers with the information they need to manage traffic flow around the rail system and to recognize and respond to one-time events such as isolated equipment failures.

Data Management. Data polled from the field units are incorporated into a real-time database that describes the current state of the Metrorail system. The AIM software interprets and uses those data to implement automatic train routing and to exercise supervisory control. At the end of each hour, all polled data are stored in AIM historical files that are automatically copied to a reporting server where they can then be used to create customized reports as needed.[44] The historical files include all status and control changes, event and alarm logs, and AIM train-tracking information. These files record only the changes to each parameter. A separate snapshot file provides the state of each parameter at the start of each hour. The files are indexed to allow quick access to all changes for specific devices over any time period.

The system can generate general reports that provide a chronology of device status or control changes across the rail system, or it can produce custom reports to identify patterns or to highlight areas of particular interest. Such specialized reports include the loss-of-shunt[45] software tool, train progress charts, train occupancy strip charts, TWC reports,[46] and system performance on-time summary (SPOTS) reports.[47] An electrical signal injected into the rails is used to determine whether a train is occupying a particular track segment. A train's wheels will "shunt" this electrical signal, alerting the signal system that a train is present. A shunt test is used by technicians to form an electrical bridge to simulate the presence of a train's wheelset in the circuit.

---

[44] These files can be copied to the reporting server manually if a report is needed before the end of the hour.

[45] The loss-of-shunt tool is a software algorithm that is used to analyze historical track occupancy data to identify track circuit anomalies.

[46] A TWC report provides the occupancy status of a platform track circuit, the preceding track circuit, and the following track circuit, along with other information reported to the central computer by the remote terminal unit, including train identification, destination, length, program station stop profile status, train master controller status (manual or automatic), ATP status (cut in or cut out), left and right door status (open or closed), train berthing status, train motion (greater than 3 mph), and door activation status (automatic or manual).

[47] A SPOTS report shows the following: the identification, destination, and length for each train moving through a station platform; the time the head of the train arrived and the rear of the train left the station; whether doors were opened; and whether door operation was detected through TWC. A SPOTS report also notes the timing for the first door opened and the last door closed.

Rail System Status Display. The LCD screens at an OCC controller console are programmed to display the current state of rail system devices and train traffic for the territory under the authority of the controllers at that console. Figure 7 is a typical display showing the status of signals, interlockings, track circuit occupancies, and train movements between the Takoma and Fort Totten stations. Based on AIM data, a typical display uses symbols to create a graphic representation of a section of the rail system and the current state of various system elements. The screens also display alarm messages in the event of certain status changes or train tracking errors. The amount of information included in the display can be adjusted as necessary to reduce clutter.

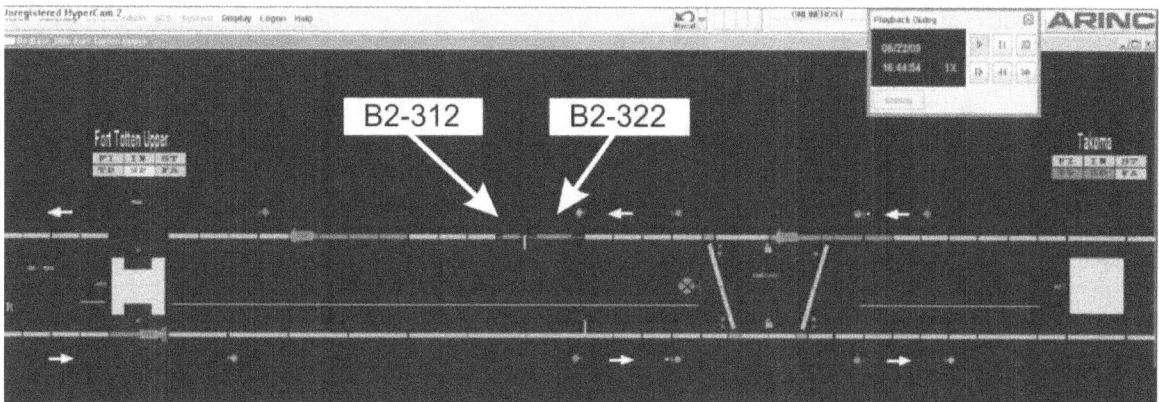

Figure 7. Example of Advanced Information Management controller display showing status of signals, interlockings, track circuit occupancies, and train movements between Fort Totten and Takoma stations. Contiguous solid red blocks indicate presence of a train. (Icons for track circuits B2-312 and B2-322 indicate that these track circuits are reporting as occupied without a train present.)

On the OCC display, main line track is depicted as a linked row of colored rectangles, with each rectangle representing a separate track circuit. The rectangle representing an unoccupied block of track (no train present) is colored gray. An occupied block is colored red. Other colors and shapes are used to indicate other track conditions. The presence of a train is indicated by a string of red (occupied) blocks with a red arrow superimposed at one end showing the train number, the operating mode (manual or automatic), and the direction of travel. Wayside signals are depicted as circular icons that indicate red or green depending on the status of the signal.

Track Occupancy Interpretation and Train Tracking. The inbound main track (track B2) between the Takoma and Fort Totten stations is divided into 27 track circuits. The automatic block system detects trains as they occupy and vacate each of these track circuits and transmits this information through remote terminal units to the AIM computer system at the OCC. The track circuit at the site of the collision is designated B2-304.

In the OCC, the AIM system, based on patterns of track occupancy for adjacent track circuits, generates train location and progress information for display on OCC controllers' screens. The AIM software will generally interpret any newly appearing contiguous group of track circuit occupancies as an as-yet-unidentified virtual train. Then, using TWC data collected from trains as they pass through a station, the system tags these virtual trains with a train number, a destination, and an operating mode. In general, the software will attach the tag information to the next virtual train in the direction of travel from a particular TWC reporting point.

The AIM system is designed to display, and in some cases sound, an alarm whenever certain patterns are detected in track occupancy data. In general, alarms that are classified as "major" must be acknowledged by the appropriate line controllers and be manually deleted (usually by the Metrorail maintenance operations center [MOC], which is a separate console within the OCC). Typically, alarms classified as "minor" can be manually acknowledged and deleted in the same manner as major alarms, but if a minor alarm remains unacknowledged after 60 seconds, the computer will automatically acknowledge and delete it.

When the AIM software detects that a normal main line track circuit is reporting as occupied in isolation (neither in front of nor behind a train), it issues a "track-circuit-failed-occupied" train tracking alarm. This alarm causes the display symbol for that track circuit to change from the normal gray to a red always-reporting block (ARB) icon. In figure 7, track circuits B2-312 and B2-322 are represented by red ARB symbols, indicating that at that moment, both track circuits were reporting as occupied even though the AIM computer algorithm had determined that they were actually vacant. According to OCC records, track-circuit-failed-occupied alarms occur at the rate of about 5,000 per week.[48]

When the AIM software detects that a track circuit reports as unoccupied under certain preprogrammed conditions, it issues a "track-circuit-failed-vacant" train tracking alarm. This alarm causes the display symbol for that track circuit to change from gray to a white non-reporting block (NRB) icon. The algorithm used to trigger an NRB alarm may be described as follows: The AIM system creates a virtual train whenever two adjacent track circuits indicate simultaneous occupancy. If one or two new track-circuit occupancy indications then occur "downstream" (in the direction of travel) of the virtual train, any intermediate track circuit that indicates "unoccupied" will generate an NRB alarm. If both previously occupied track circuits indicate "unoccupied" without the track circuit downstream from these indicating "occupied," both of the previously occupied track circuits will generate NRB alarms. If a train occupies three or more track circuits and one or more of the intermediate track circuits indicates "unoccupied," those unoccupied track circuits will generate NRB alarms. These NRB track circuits will be depicted on the OCC display with a white icon. According to OCC records, NRB track-circuit-failed-vacant alarms occur at the rate of about 3,000 per week.[49]

The AIM software responds to a "bobbing" track circuit (a track circuit malfunction in which a track circuit transitions from vacant, to occupied, to vacant again with no train traffic

---

[48] About 100 track circuits (of about 3,000 track circuits systemwide) account for the majority of the ARB track-circuit-failed-occupied alarms.

[49] The same track circuits that account for the majority of the ARB track-circuit-failed-occupied alarms also account for the majority of the NRB track-circuit-failed-vacant alarms.

present) by issuing a cascade of track-circuit-failed-occupied/failed-vacant alarms. Because of the high incidence of bobbing track circuit alarms, WMATA has designated track-circuit-failed-occupied/failed-vacant alarms as minor alarms. Loss of train detection is a different type of track circuit malfunction, which will be discussed later.

In the event that all track occupancy indications disappear under a virtual train and do not reappear within 30 seconds, the AIM software will delete the virtual train image without generating an alarm. This feature is designed to eliminate nuisance, or "ghost," trains (virtual trains created by the train tracking system that have no coincidence with actual trains) that are created as a result of bobbing track circuits. Additional algorithms not described in this report are used to eliminate ghost trains. According to OCC records, the AIM system creates and then deletes more than 1,000 ghost trains each week.

OCC Controller Displays During Accident Sequence

Using the archived AIM historical data for the track segment between the Takoma and Fort Totten stations, investigators recreated and reviewed the screen displays available to OCC Ops. 1 console controllers on the day of the accident. From these displays the series of graphics shown in appendix B was developed. Each graphic presents an enlarged view of a section of the screen display that includes the accident trains as they would have been displayed to the OCC controllers during the accident sequence.

Signal Information

Train Detection and Collision Avoidance

The ATP subsystem, working in conjunction with properly operating train equipment, is intended to provide protection against collisions and train overspeed. The wayside portion of the ATP subsystem includes the automatic block system (discussed below) and control of track switches and signals.

The automatic block system detects trains as they occupy and vacate each of these track circuits and, if necessary, transmits speed commands (including a command of 0 mph) to following trains to maintain train separation. Track occupancy information is also transmitted through remote terminal units to the AIM system at the OCC. The algorithm used to compute speed commands does not take into account any information regarding the past status of track occupancies or speed commands.

Track occupancy detection is accomplished as follows: At each end of each track circuit, an impedance bond is mounted between the rails. (See figure 8.) The impedance bond at one end of the block acts as a transmitter; the one at the other end acts as a receiver.[50] Track circuits are typically arranged for the normal direction of traffic so that a train entering a track circuit will pass over the receiver end of a track circuit before traversing the transmitter end.

Figure 8. Impedance bond for track circuit B2-304.

A track circuit transmitter module in the train control room generates a code-rate modulated audio frequency signal and supplies it to the transmitter impedance bond at the end of a track circuit. The transmitter impedance bond injects this signal into the rails. Assuming that no train occupies the block, the signal will travel through the rails and be picked up by the receiver impedance bond at the other end of the track circuit. The receiver bond sends this signal back to

---

[50] Only one impedance bond is mounted at the junction of two track circuits. Generally, this single impedance bond serves as the receiver for one track circuit and the transmitter for the adjacent "upstream" track circuit.

a track circuit receiver module in the train control room. (See figure 9.) The track circuit receiver module filters, amplifies, and checks the level of the signal it receives from the impedance bond. If the signal meets the amplitude and modulation requirements for that track circuit, the module energizes the coil of a track relay. The energized coil causes the relay armature to "pick up," or rise, thus completing the track circuit. A track relay in the "up," or raised, position indicates to the ATC system that the block of track is unoccupied.

Figure 9. Typical track circuit module.

When a train enters the track circuit, the train's wheelsets provide an alternative path for the signal and shunt[51] it away from the receiver bond. When the code-rate modulated signal being sent by the receiver bond back to the track circuit receiver module drops below a preset level, the module deenergizes the corresponding track relay, causing the relay armature to drop, signifying that a train is occupying the track circuit. After the last wheels of a train leave the track circuit, the signal again reaches the receiver bond, causing the track relay to pick up, signifying an unoccupied block. The process works the same way on both main tracks regardless of the direction of travel. A loss of train detection occurs when the relay does not deenergize while a train is occupying the track circuit.

---

[51] Shunting actually occurs shortly before a train arrives at the track circuit (preshunting) and remains in effect until briefly after a train has moved out of the track circuit (postshunting).

Postaccident Inspection and Testing of ATP Components

Control of 14 of the 27 track circuits along track B2 between the Takoma and Fort Totten stations is provided by track circuit modules containing plug-in printed circuit boards mounted on equipment racks in the Fort Totten train control room.[52] Based on serial numbers and WMATA records, the ATP transmitter/receiver modules installed at Fort Totten at the time of the accident were manufactured by GRS[53] in the early 1970s. Some modules had been replaced since the original installation with modules of the same or similar design (early 1970s to late 1980s), and some of the components used in the modules, such as printed circuit boards, also had been changed since the original installation.[54]

The collision occurred within a 738-foot-long track circuit designated B2-304, located about 1/2 mile north of the Fort Totten station. Postaccident examination of the equipment revealed that the track relay for track circuit B2-304 was out of correspondence with the physical location of the accident trains. That is, the track relay was energized (indicating a vacant track circuit) even though both accident trains were still occupying the block and shunting the track circuit.

The postaccident inspection conducted on June 23, 2009, did not find any indications of tampering with or vandalism of the train control system. After the accident wreckage was removed, investigators tested the five track circuits preceding (north to south)[55] track circuit B2-304 using a 0.06-ohm shunt to simulate a train wheelset. Investigators sequentially placed the shunt at three locations—at the transmitter end, in the middle, and at the receiver end—of each track circuit. All track relays deenergized in response to the placement of each shunt. Investigators then tested track circuit B2-304. The track circuit detected a 0.06-ohm shunt placed at the transmitter end of the circuit but failed to detect either a 0.06-ohm or a hardwire shunt[56] placed in the middle of the circuit. When either type of shunt (0.06 ohm or hardwire) was placed at the receiver end of the track circuit, detection of the shunt was intermittent; the track relay momentarily energized and picked up (showed "unoccupied"), and then deenergized and dropped out (showed "occupied").

The NTSB tested the B2-304 vital, or safety-critical, track circuit relay, along with other associated vital relays, for compliance with performance criteria. All 15 vital relays were found

---

[52] The remaining 13 track circuits are controlled from Takoma.

[53] GRS is General Railway Signal Company, which has since been acquired by Alstom Signaling Inc. In this report, "GRS" will be used when referring to the signal system components themselves; "Alstom" will be used when referring to the company providing technical support for the GRS components.

[54] According to Alstom, since the 1970s, Alstom's GRS ATC modules have evolved over four "generations." The modules in use at Fort Totten were Generation 2 modules. The company does not believe that any Generation 1 modules remain in service.

[55] From north to south, the tested track circuits were B2-344, B2-336, B2-328, B2-322, and B2-312.

[56] A hardwire shunt is a near-zero resistance wire as opposed to a 0.06-ohm shunt that is used to simulate the axle of the train.

to be operating within specifications. The two US&S[57] impedance bonds (transmitter and receiver) for track circuit B2-304 were electronically swept to check the tuning frequency and were determined to be in compliance with manufacturer specifications. The US&S transmitter bond for track B2-304 had been installed on June 16 and 17, 2009, to replace a GRS impedance bond. (As discussed elsewhere in this report, the bond was installed as part of a WMATA long-term track-circuit replacement program.) During this investigation, the newly installed US&S transmitter impedance bond was removed for inspection and bench testing. No exceptions were noted with the condition or operation of the US&S impedance bond.

Postaccident testing determined that the US&S impedance bond had a resistive impedance of 132.6 ohms versus a resistive impedance of 140.6 ohms for the replaced GRS impedance bond. Because of this difference in impedance, the installation of a US&S impedance bond in a track circuit with GRS transmitter and receiver modules in some cases required that the track circuit transmitter power be changed during the subsequent track circuit adjustment and verification process. In postaccident interviews, WMATA ATC technicians said that transmitter power levels had to be increased about one-third of the time when US&S impedance bonds were used with GRS track circuit modules.

Postaccident testing conducted by the NTSB detected signal coupling between the ATP track circuit transmitter and receiver modules that contributed to energizing the B2-304 track relay (indicating "vacant") while the track circuit was actually occupied. This testing identified parasitic oscillation[58] generated by the power output transistors of the track-circuit transmitter. This oscillation produced a spurious track-circuit signal that was picked up by the track-circuit receiver and interpreted as the nonshunted signal coming from the receiver impedance bond. The parasitic oscillation was generated by the transmitter module and coupled through the heat sinks[59] and through the rack and module structures to other modules that shared the same power source and rack. The amplitude of the oscillation was found to vary significantly depending on the transmitter power level setting. For example, during testing of the Fort Totten modules, when the transmitter power level was increased from 55 percent (the setting at the time of the accident) to 60 percent, the parasitic oscillation did not cause a loss of train detection. When the power level was reduced from 60 percent to 30 percent (the power level before the impedance bond was replaced), the oscillation also did not cause a loss of train detection. The oscillation was present both when the US&S impedance bonds were included in the circuit and when the bonds were disconnected and replaced with a simulated load. Testing of other modules showed that the oscillation could appear at times after an increase in transmitter power level and at other times after a reduction in the power level.

The oscillation was not continuous and only occurred when a power transistor signal amplitude reached a certain level. The oscillation occurred in pulses that were driven by the audio frequency signal. Because the oscillation was affected by the signal amplitude, it was only

---

[57] US&S refers to Union Switch & Signal, which changed its name to Ansaldo STS USA, Inc., on January 1, 2009. In this report, "US&S" will be used when referring to the signal system components themselves; "Ansaldo" will be used when referring to the company providing technical support for the US&S components.

[58] In this instance, *parasitic oscillation* refers to spurious signal pulses generated by the power amplifier.

[59] A *heat sink* is a heat exchanger designed to absorb and to dissipate excess heat.

present when the track circuit was transmitting; therefore, the oscillation was synchronized with the coded signal injected into the track. Once the oscillation was coupled to the module containing the track circuit receiver, the power amplifier for the adjacent track circuit module amplified the pulses. The amplified pulses were coupled to the track circuit receiver detector, where the pulses were interpreted to be the correct audio frequency signal for that track circuit. When the amplitude of the pulses was sufficient, the receiver amplifier provided output to the relay driver, which energized the track relay (signifying an unoccupied track).

On August 7, 2009, in an attempt to eliminate such parasitic oscillation, WMATA asked for Alstom's approval to modify a printed circuit board on the GRS track circuit modules. Alstom replied on August 31, 2009, that it had not had the opportunity to independently analyze and test the proposed modification and was therefore unable to approve the WMATA plan. On September 4, 2009, WMATA informed Alstom that it would not pursue the proposed circuit modification without Alstom's approval.

On August 9, 2009, WMATA engineers completed draft ATC technical procedure T163, *GRS ATP Module Parasitic Oscillation Test*. In August and September 2009, WMATA engineering personnel, using the draft T163 test procedure, began testing other track circuits on the Metrorail system for the type of parasitic oscillation that was found at Fort Totten. The initial testing focused on track circuits identified by the loss-of-shunt tool as having timing anomalies.[60] The testing was expanded to include track circuits that had not shown timing anomalies but that were located in the same train control rooms as circuits specifically identified for testing. This initial testing involved 96 track circuits. Of these, 20 were identified as having parasitic oscillation coupled between the transmitter and receiver modules like that found at Fort Totten. The 20 track circuits were all equipped with GRS impedance bonds and GRS track circuit modules.

On September 22, 2009, the NTSB made the following urgent safety recommendation to WMATA:

> Examine track circuits within your system that may be susceptible to parasitic oscillation and spurious signals capable of exploiting unintended signal paths, and eliminate those adverse conditions that could affect the safe performance of your train control system. This work should be conducted in coordination with your signal and train control equipment manufacturer(s). (R-09-15 Urgent)

---

[60] During this time, WMATA was refining the accuracy of its loss-of-shunt tool. Therefore, although all of the identified track circuits were investigated, not all of them were found to have loss-of-shunt anomalies; corrugated rail was identified at some locations.

After, and in partial response to, the issuance of Safety Recommendation R-09-15, draft test procedure T163 was made final on October 21, 2009. The final test procedure identifies four types of oscillations:

> 4.1 <u>Oscillation type 1</u>: Look for a <u>clean sinusoidal audio waveform</u>. If none of the audio waveform appearance is thickened by higher frequency oscillations, then enter the number "1" in column 2 of the data sheet. The failure mode is not present for the tested track circuit and your test of this track circuit is complete.

> 4.2 <u>Oscillation type 2</u>: If the entire waveform appears uniformly thickened as though it is out of focus, that indicates a harmless and <u>continuous oscillation</u> at some higher frequency .... This phenomenon may be present with other phenomena described below and if there is excessive amplitude of continuous oscillation, it might mask other oscillation types. If other bulges representing periodic bursts of oscillation appear on the waveform, then look for type 3 or type 4 oscillations. If the continuous oscillation, is the only oscillation, then record the number "2" in column 2, the measured frequency in column 3, and the measured amplitude in column 4. The failure mode is not present for the tested track circuit and your test of this track circuit is complete.

> 4.3 <u>Oscillation type 3</u>: If the thickened portions of the waveform are consistently and only in the same region (usually at a positive and/or negative peak) then the thickened regions are <u>local oscillations of the shared track circuit transmitter</u>. The shared track circuit may be at risk for the parasitic oscillation failure mode, but if there are no other pulses of oscillation then the tested track circuit does not have the failure mode. ... The failure mode is not present for the tested track circuit and your test of this track circuit is complete. However, you should begin tests of the shared track circuit immediately beginning at step #1.

> 4.4 <u>Oscillation type 4</u>: If the thickened portions of the waveform are irregular with respect to the audio frequency of the shared track circuit, (they appear at different angles/locations of the waveform) then they are coming from another transmitter, via the power distribution and rack structures, and are superimposed on the preamp of the shared track circuit transmitter. These are <u>external oscillations for the shared track circuit transmitter</u>. It is important to determine the source of these "pulses" that appear as thickened portions on the audio waveform.

The test procedure requires corrective action when the amplitude of the type 4 oscillation exceeds and remains above 400 millivolts. Screen captures of oscilloscope displays illustrating the four types of parasitic oscillation are shown in figure 10.

After the T163 test procedure became final, WMATA ATC personnel were trained to identify oscillation using the procedure. From the end of October through the end of December 2009, technicians tested 1,482 track circuits throughout the Metrorail system and found 208 track circuits having type 3 parasitic oscillation that was being generated in the transmitter track circuit module but was not seen in the receiver modules. That testing identified an additional 82 track circuits that exhibited type 4 oscillation with parasitic oscillation in both the transmitter and receiver modules. Only eight of these had oscillation with signal strength deemed sufficient by WMATA to require corrective action. In those eight cases, the oscillation could be mitigated by adjusting the track circuit transmitter power level setting. All 82 track circuits that were identified as having type 4 oscillation like that found at Fort Totten used GRS impedance bonds and GRS track circuit modules.

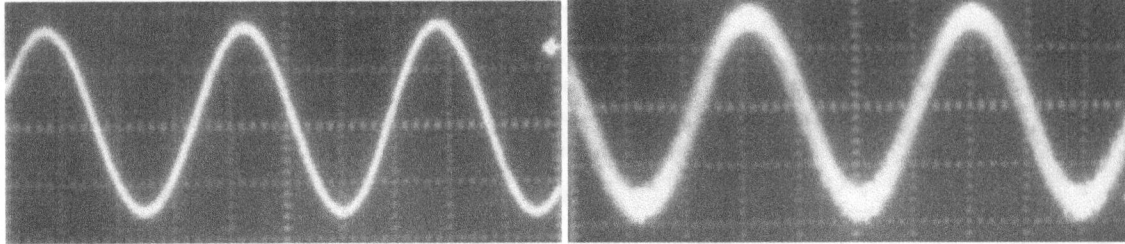

Oscillation type 1: A clean sinusoidal audio waveform.

Oscillation type 2: The entire waveform appears uniformly thickened as though out of focus. Indicates a harmless and continuous oscillation at some higher frequency (25 megahertz for example).

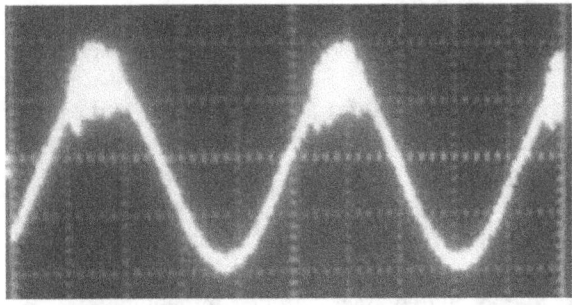
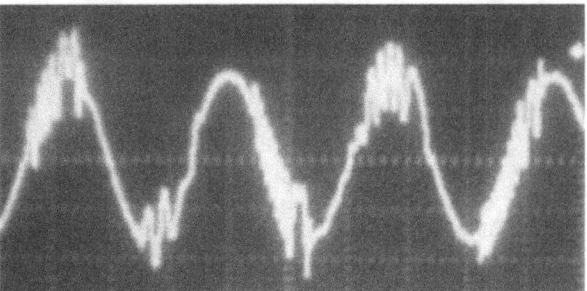

Oscillation type 3: The thickened portions of the waveform are all in the same region (usually at a positive or negative peak), indicating local (internal) oscillations. The track circuit may be at risk for the parasitic oscillation failure mode.

Oscillation type 4: The thickened portions of the waveform are irregular (they appear at different angles/locations of the waveform), indicating that they are coming from another transmitter, via the power distribution and rack structures, and are superimposed on the preamplifier of the shared track circuit transmitter. These are external oscillations that could mimic a valid track circuit signal and result in a loss of train detection.

Figure 10. Oscilloscope displays illustrating four types of parasitic oscillation found in WMATA GRS track circuit modules. (Source: WMATA technical procedure T163, *GRS ATP Module Parasitic Oscillation Test*.)

Metrorail Upgrade Program Activities

Traction Power Upgrade Program

Metrorail train traction power is supplied through an electrified third rail that provides 750 volts to the traction motors aboard each car. The Red Line traction power system could accommodate 6-car trains, but with increased Metrorail ridership, WMATA began a program to upgrade traction power substations in preparation for operating 8-car trains. The New Hampshire Avenue traction power substation, near the accident site, was upgraded from 4 megawatts to 7 megawatts between March 7 and June 14, 2006. The upgrade entailed replacing two 2-megawatt transformers with two new 2-megawatt transformers and adding a new 3-megawatt transformer.

Track Circuit Replacement Program

At the time of the accident, WMATA was also working on a program to replace the GRS track circuits in selected locations. According to WMATA's former ATC assistant chief engineer's testimony at the public hearing, the track circuit replacement program was needed because the track circuits had aged, some of the parts were failing, and replacement parts were not available. The program called for GRS impedance bonds and GRS track circuit modules to be replaced with US&S impedance bonds and US&S AF-800W modules. The track circuit replacement program was managed by the WMATA Metrorail Infrastructure Renewal Programs Group and involved ATC construction, inspection, and testing (CIT) crews from Metrorail's office of Track Structures System Maintenance (TSSM).

The program was being carried out in the following sequence: First, WMATA CIT crews would replace the GRS impedance bonds with US&S bonds. The CIT crews would make any necessary adjustments to the affected track circuits and verify that the circuits were working properly with the new bonds. Once this was complete, an Ansaldo crew, with assistance from WMATA, would install the US&S modules in the train control room and make final track circuit adjustments. According to WMATA officials, WMATA attempted to have its bond replacement crews working one station ahead of the Ansaldo crews.

The first track circuit replacement contract was for three locations on the Orange line. On October 6, 2006, the office of the WMATA chief engineer issued an engineering bulletin titled *US&S Impedance Bonds in GRS ATP Track Circuits* that stated that no problems had been reported with the three Orange Line installations in which US&S impedance bonds had been installed in track circuits that still used GRS components. The bulletin continued as follows:

> Verification with a .06 ohm shunt is WMATA's worst case shunting condition. Verification Shunt Test should be performed at each end of the track circuit and at the mid point in the track circuit. Any track circuit that verifies with a .06 ohm shunt is considered safe. This same procedure will be used to set up any track circuit in which

WMATA will replace a GRS impedance bond with a US&S impedance bond with GRS ATP Modules. If during the installation and testing the track circuit cannot be adjusted to pass a .06 ohm verification shunt test then the old GRS bond should be reinstalled.

Replacement of Impedance Bonds Near Fort Totten

On December 12, 2007, as part of the traction power upgrade program, the GRS impedance bond at chain marker B2-311+71 was replaced with a US&S high-current bond. The replaced impedance bond was the receiver impedance bond for track circuit B2-304 (the site of the accident on the inbound track, north of Fort Totten station) and the transmitter impedance bond for track circuit B2-312 (the track circuit immediately north of B2-304).

According to the daily entry for that date in the Fort Totten train control room log, a track circuit adjustment was performed on track circuits B2-312 and B2-304 after the US&S impedance bond was installed. The log also indicated that a shunt verification test was performed and that the power level was raised from 55 to 70 percent for track circuit B2-312.

On December 18, 2007, also as part of the traction power upgrade program, the GRS receiver impedance bond for track circuit B1-245 (on the outbound track, south of Fort Totten station) was replaced with a US&S high-current impedance bond. The transmitter power level was increased, and although the track circuit was reportedly adjusted and verified, recorded data show that the track circuit repeatedly lost detection of trains after the bond replacement.

On December 24, 2007, a work order was opened for track circuit B1-245. The log book entry for that date stated that track circuit B1-245 would not shunt with a train in the circuit. Records show that the track circuit was adjusted and verified, but recorded data reviewed during the investigation show that the track circuit repeatedly lost detection of trains after the adjustment.

On January 10, 2008, the entry in the log book indicated that track circuit B1-245 was still not consistently detecting trains. The transmitter power level setting was changed, but technicians could not adjust the track circuit such that the track relay would remain energized. A CIT crew inspected the track circuit and changed the transmitter power level, but they too were unable to adjust the track circuit to function properly. At that point, the ATC technicians removed track circuit B1-245 from service and notified the OCC and the MOC.

The next day, the transmitter power level for track circuit B1-245 was changed again, but the track circuit still could not be adjusted to function properly. Another work order was opened. The following day, January 12, 2008, technicians removed the US&S high-current impedance bond that had been installed on December 18, 2007, and reinstalled the original GRS impedance bond. The track circuit was adjusted and verified after increasing the transmitter power level. An NTSB review of historical data from the loss-of-shunt tool indicated that track circuit B1-245 continued to lose train detection after the original bond was reinstalled.

A review by WMATA ATC engineers of track circuit adjustment data for track circuit B1-245 indicated that the transmitter voltage level had been decreasing from May 2006 to August 2008. Based on this finding, the engineers determined that the GRS transmitter impedance bond for the track circuit was defective. On September 9, 2008, the GRS transmitter impedance bond for track circuit B1-245 was replaced with another GRS impedance bond. The track circuit was adjusted and verified. A review of historical data showed that the track circuit continued to fail to detect trains.

As the traction power upgrade program was nearing completion, a review by WMATA noted that track circuit B1-245 (because of the problems involving loss of train detection) still had the original GRS receiver impedance bond. On January 10, 2009, the GRS receiver impedance bond was again replaced with a US&S high-current impedance bond. On April 20, 2009, the GRS transmitter impedance bond for this track circuit was replaced with a US&S impedance bond. The track circuit was adjusted and verified after each of these US&S impedance bond installations, and no changes were made in transmitter power level. The historical data revealed that track circuit B1-245 continued to lose train detection after both impedance bond replacements.

On August 14, 2009, the GRS track circuit modules were replaced with US&S modules. A review of the historical records from August 15, 2009, through January 1, 2010, showed no further loss-of-shunt events involving track circuit B1-245.

Five days before the accident, as part of the WMATA track circuit replacement program, a WMATA CIT crew replaced the original GRS transmitter impedance bond for track circuit B2-304 with a US&S impedance bond. The GRS track circuit modules in the Fort Totten train control room were scheduled to be replaced with US&S AF-800W modules during the week of June 22, 2009.

The CIT crew leader for the installation of the US&S impedance bond told investigators that after her crew installed the new bond, they experienced problems while making track circuit adjustments and had to increase transmitter power from 30 to 55 percent before they could get the receiver track relay to pick up. She stated that during the adjustments, track circuit B2-304 began bobbing (transitioning from showing vacant to occupied and back to vacant with no traffic present).

The crew leader stated that during the track adjustment, her crew performed a shunt verification test at three points along the B2-304 track circuit. She stated that the track circuit detected each of the three shunts. The crew leader stated that for preventive maintenance track circuit verification, they were only required to use one shunt placed 10 feet inside the transmitter end, but for replacement of an impedance bond and track circuit verification, her preference (not a requirement) was to shunt in three places on the track circuit.

Data from the morning of June 17, 2009, (obtained after the accident) indicated that track circuit B2-304 was performing irregularly during the time the track circuit adjustment and verification process was conducted. Because of the frequent bobbing of track circuit B2-304, the data could not be used to confirm the CIT crew leader's statements made during the postaccident interview regarding the use of three shunts to verify the track circuit. NTSB postaccident testing of track circuit B2-304 determined that the track circuit detected a 0.06-ohm shunt at the transmitter end of the circuit. However, the track circuit failed to detect a 0.06-ohm or a hardwire shunt in the middle of the track circuit. With a shunt (0.06-ohm or hardwire) at the receiver end, the track circuit was intermittently detecting the shunt, momentarily deenergizing the relay and then energizing the relay and not detecting the shunt.

The installation crew completed the installation and adjustments just before the start of revenue service on the morning of June 17, 2009. The crew leader said that she spoke with her supervisor by telephone about the problems her crew had encountered when making adjustments and that he had instructed them to stay and observe two train movements before departing. The crew leader stated that as they waited for trains to begin running, track circuit B2-304 began bobbing again. They replaced the relay driver card, but the track circuit continued bobbing.

The crew leader said that the track circuit properly detected the first revenue train that went through. (Recorded track circuit data indicated that track circuit B2-304 failed to detect the first train.) She said after the train departed the area, track circuit B2-304 continued to bob, and the adjacent track circuit B2-312 also began bobbing. Personnel from the Metrorail MOC called the crew at the Fort Totten train control room to notify them of the bobbing track circuits and were told that the crew was still there and was troubleshooting the bobbing track circuits.

The crew observed a second train movement and again stated that they did not notice any problem with the train being detected as it moved through the track circuits. The crew leader said that just before 6:00 a.m., she called the MOC and reported that the crew had observed two train movements through the area and that, while they did not notice any problems with train detection, the two track circuits (B2-304 and B2-312) were still bobbing. She said that MOC personnel acknowledged the report, after which she and her crew departed the area and went off duty. The crew leader stated that the crew did not hear anything more regarding the two track circuits until 5 days later when the accident occurred.

In a postaccident interview, the supervisor of the CIT installation crew said, "If the track circuit's bobbing, normal procedure is [that it] ... be worked on. If there's a crew changeover, it's still to be worked on." He said his understanding was that when the CIT crew departed on June 17, "there was no problem." He also said he was not aware of an instance in which ATC technicians had taken a track segment out of service because of a failed verification test or a bobbing track circuit, but that

> I would have to stress to the technicians, if you have a problem with a track circuit or anything else, ... shut it down. I've done it with switches where you just call out of service. And I don't know whether that's taught to all of ATC.... If you've got a problem with it, shut it down and deal with the consequences later. The mentality now is move trains.

Records show that, as a result of reports by the CIT installation crew, the MOC opened work order No. 7169867 for bobbing track circuit B2-304 at 6:50 a.m. on June 17, 2009. Although the CIT crew leader told investigators that she had notified the MOC that both track circuits B2-304 and B2-312 were bobbing, the MOC had no work orders associated with bobbing track circuit B2-312. No incident ticket was associated with the work order for track circuit B2-304. Incident tickets are generated for unusual occurrences in the operating system and, except for temporary speed restrictions, require initiation by transportation personnel in the OCC. Work orders may be generated from incident tickets for maintenance action, but they may also be initiated without an incident.

On June 17, 2009, after the new impedance bond was installed and a work order was opened for a bobbing track circuit, Red Line ATC technicians performed a scheduled preventive maintenance inspection in the area where the collision occurred. That work included performing quarterly verification shunt tests, which they believed involved placing a single 0.06-ohm shunt 10 feet inside the track circuit at the transmitter end. They said that track circuit B2-304 detected the shunt but that when their testing was complete, the circuit was bobbing. They stated that they then measured the line voltage and compared the measurements to historical records of the circuit. The measurements were found to be consistent with the historical records. The ATC technicians said that after they completed this troubleshooting, they did not make any adjustments because the track circuit had just been verified with the shunt test, indicating to them that it was safe. They said they did not report the bobbing track circuit to the MOC because the problem cleared itself while they were troubleshooting. They said they were not aware of the open work order regarding track circuit B2-304.

No action was taken regarding work order No. 7169867 from the time it was opened on June 17, 2009, until the day of the accident. ATC shift supervisors are responsible for reviewing open work orders for their areas of responsibility. TSSM managers also review open incident tickets to ensure that they are properly handled. Because work order No. 7169867 was not associated with an incident ticket, it was never included in any list that TSSM managers reviewed.

At the public hearing on this accident, the WMATA superintendent of communications stated that between June 17 and June 22, 2009, 39 preventive maintenance work orders and 9 corrective maintenance work orders were completed. He said that most of the completed maintenance work orders had to do with problems that prevented OCC controllers from being able to set a route for trains. He stated that any required maintenance action that affects train movements takes priority.

Investigators reviewed incident tickets and work orders for the area between Fort Totten and Takoma dating back 18 months before the accident. The records indicated that on February 28, 2008, work order No. 4397137 was opened for track circuit B2-304, which was bobbing. The records indicated that work was completed on September 6, 2008, and the work order was closed on September 26, 2008. The work order entries did not indicate the actions that had been taken to correct the bobbing track circuit.

Review of ATC Recorded Data

NTSB investigators reviewed the AIM system historical data records regarding track circuit B2-304. The records indicated that about 1:33 a.m. on December 12, 2007, track circuit B2-304 was down. The data corresponded to the date and time the high-current impedance bond (the B2-304 track circuit receiver bond) was replaced. The data further indicated that about 5 hours later, track circuit B2-304 began bobbing by showing false train occupancies between train movements. The track circuit detected actual trains but at times falsely indicated occupancy when no train was present.

The historical records indicated that the intermittent indications of false train occupancy for track circuit B2-304 were still occurring when the track circuit transmitter impedance bond was replaced on June 17, 2009. The records showed that during the time the installation crew was carrying out the postinstallation track circuit adjustment and verification process for the new impedance bond, the track circuit continued to perform irregularly. From the time the impedance bond was replaced until shortly before the arrival of the first train of the day, the track circuit was bobbing, and the track circuit relay was seldom energized (indicating a vacant circuit) for more than 30 seconds between dropouts. Then, about 9 minutes before the arrival of the first train, the track circuit relay began to remain energized for minutes at a time and was only bobbing (intermittently indicating an occupied track circuit) for a second or two. The data further indicated that train detection failed for almost every train that occupied track circuit B2-304 from the time the impedance bond was replaced on June 17, 2009, until the accident on June 22. No record was found that any train operator had reported losing speed commands at the accident location in the 5 days leading up to the accident.

Investigators determined that, on the day of the accident, almost all of the inbound trains departing Takoma toward Fort Totten operated on proper speed commands to maintain train separation until they entered track circuit B2-304, at which time their speed commands dropped to 0 mph. As the trains slowed in response to the 0 mph speed command, they coasted through track circuit B2-304 and onto track circuit B2-301, the next track circuit in the direction of travel. When the train was detected by track circuit B2-301, the ATC system again transmitted proper speed commands, and the trains continued normally. This sequence continued until the time of the accident.

The AIM system would have issued an alarm each time track circuit B2-304 provided a false occupancy or false vacancy indication, and these alarms would have been displayed on the line controller screens in the OCC. Because WMATA had identified such alarms as "minor," the alarm messages would have appeared briefly on the screen display before being automatically acknowledged and deleted by the AIM system without controller intervention. The red or white icons representing an ARB or NRB track circuit would have continued to be displayed on the primary screens even after the alarm messages had been deleted. These icons would have been replaced by the normal track circuit icons during those periods when the track circuit was performing normally or when a latent malfunction could not be detected by the ATC system.

Recorded train control system data indicated that, minutes before the accident, train 214 entered track circuit B2-312 with speed commands of 55 mph. As the train approached (preshunted) track circuit B2-304, the speed commands were reduced to 45 mph because of the presence of train 110 that was approaching Fort Totten station ahead of train 214. As train 214 continued moving onto track circuit B2-304, its presence stopped being detected. Because speed commands are only transmitted when a track circuit is occupied, the train received no speed commands, which resulted in default speed readouts of 0 mph. This caused train 214 to stop fully within the limits of track circuit B2-304.

Previous Metrorail Incident Involving Failure of Train Detection

In 2005, a track circuit failed to detect the presence of stopped trains on the outbound track between the Foggy Bottom and Rosslyn stations. Because of these failures, the operators of two trains had to override the ATO system and stop their trains to prevent a rear-end collision. The circumstances of that incident, as related by Metrorail officials during the February 2010 public hearing on this accident, were as follows:

Metrorail trains, except for Red Line trains, share the same tracks for significant portions of their routes. (Refer to figure 2.) In areas where two Metrorail lines are shown running in parallel, they share the same main line track. For example, both Orange Line and Blue Line trains use the same track between Stadium-Armory and Rosslyn. At Rosslyn, based on the train identification as detected by the TWC system, the ATC system automatically aligns switches so that, after serving the Rosslyn station, outbound trains are routed either toward Vienna (Orange Line trains) or Franconia-Springfield (Blue Line trains).

On June 7, 2005, because of a failure in the TWC system, trains departing Rosslyn had to be routed manually by the OCC rather than automatically from the wayside. During the evening rush period, an OCC controller misrouted an outbound train from Rosslyn, which caused a backup of following outbound Blue and Orange Line trains between the Foggy Bottom and Rosslyn stations.

The backup resulted in a train being stopped within track circuit C2-111, a 900-foot-long track circuit at about the midpoint between Rosslyn and Foggy Bottom stations. The ATP subsystem failed to detect the presence of the train in the track circuit, which allowed speed commands to be transmitted to the train immediately behind the stopped train. When the operator of that train, who was operating in ATO, saw the train ahead and realized that his train was not slowing, he used his ATO stop button (a non-emergency brake application) to apply the train brakes. He estimated that his train stopped about 50 feet short of the rear of the stopped train. The operator believed he had a problem with speed commands, which he reported to the OCC.

Eventually, the first train moved forward, and the train that had stopped to prevent a collision moved ahead until it was now occupying the track circuit previously occupied by the first train. Track circuit C2-111 again failed to detect the presence of the train, which allowed speed commands to be transmitted to the following train. The operator of the following train, who was also operating in ATO, saw the train ahead, determined that he was moving too fast, and applied his train's emergency brakes. He estimated that his train stopped about 20 feet short of the rear of the other train.

About 1.5 hours later, a WMATA ATC engineer, while discussing with the MOC the information he would need to address the failure in the TWC system at Rosslyn, overheard someone referring to the incident involving emergency brakes being applied because of excessive speed in the tunnel between Rosslyn and Foggy Bottom. He asked for more data regarding the incident and contacted other ATC engineers.

Three ATC engineers reviewed the computer data for the track circuits and determined that the near-collisions had resulted from a failure of track circuit C2-111 to detect the presence of a train in the middle of the circuit. They immediately established absolute block[61] protection for the track circuit and began investigating the cause.

The engineers conducted a number of tests and determined that the failed train detection could theoretically have resulted from an electrical fault between the transmitter and receiver impedance bond cables.[62] Such a fault could provide a "runaround" circuit that would allow a signal to travel from the track circuit transmitter to the track circuit receiver without ever reaching the rails. The engineers were unable to fully test this theory because when they cut a cable tie binding the cables together, the track circuit began detecting trains. Visual inspection of the two cables revealed no physical evidence of a short.

Additional troubleshooting followed over the next few days, as did consultation with engineers from Alstom regarding the GRS track circuit components. Although an electrical short between the cables was believed to be the most rational explanation for the failure, no definitive cause for the malfunction was ever identified. All components of the track circuit were subsequently replaced, including both the transmitter and the receiver impedance bonds, all the bond cables between the train control room and the track, and the transmitter and receiver modules in the Rosslyn train control room.

As a result of the Rosslyn incident and subsequent investigation, WMATA developed the loss-of-shunt tool. As noted previously, a train's wheels "shunt" the electrical signal injected into the rails, alerting the signal system that a train is present. The loss-of-shunt software tool is designed to scan the database for track occupancy occurrences that violate the "3-second rule." This rule is based on the assumption that a 4-car train cannot move fast enough to completely leave a single track circuit less than 3 seconds after entering the next track circuit in the direction of travel. In other words, a loss-of-shunt event occurs when a track circuit transitions to

---

[61] An *absolute block* is a section of track between two specific locations, such as passenger stations, into which no train is permitted to enter while that section of track is occupied by another train. The section of track can be of any length (that is, multiple track circuits or multiple stations). The OCC must verify with a qualified employee positioned at the limits of each block that a train authorized to occupy the absolute block has passed the limits of that block before authorizing another train to occupy the block.

[62] The two sheathed, twisted-pair cables ran parallel to and in contact with one another for about 3,100 feet along the tunnel wall.

"unoccupied" less than 3 seconds after the next track circuit transitions to "occupied." This is an indication that the track circuit, at some point, lost the ability to detect whether a train was occupying that block of track. In general, the loss-of-shunt software tool can only identify those instances in which a loss of shunt occurs under an actual train.

According to testimony given at the public hearing on this accident, ATC engineers initially used the loss-of-shunt tool on a weekly basis. After about a year, the procedures for using the loss-of-shunt tool were codified, and the tool was turned over to the maintenance department with a recommendation that it be used once per month. According to those involved in the development of the tool, the recommendation was that the tool be used to analyze a 3-hour peak service period, for the entire Metrorail system, once per month.

At the public hearing, the communications superintendent for WMATA stated that he had found no records to indicate that loss-of-shunt analyses were being performed on a monthly basis and documented. He went on to state the following:

> From the information that I was provided, I was told that it [the loss-of-shunt tool] was being run monthly. In fact, some managers in ATC informed me they were, in fact, running it weekly, but when [I] inquired as to the documentation, there was none available.

On June 19, 2005, WMATA issued an engineering bulletin and ATC safety notice: *Update on Diminished Shunt Sensitivity in Audio Frequency Track Circuits.* The bulletin states (in enlarged type)

> Shunt-verification of audio frequency track circuits, must include a 'soft' (0.06 [ohm]) shunt test at the transmitter AND in the middle of the track circuit.

> A recently discovered, non-indicating failure mode [as discovered in the Rosslyn incident] could result in near normal shunting sensitivity at the ends of the track circuit with an inability to detect trains in the middle.

The WMATA ATC systems engineer interviewed as part of the Fort Totten accident investigation also participated in the 2005 Rosslyn investigation. He said that after all the components for track circuit C2-111 were replaced, he retained the old GRS modules and kept them in his office for further examination. He stated that he performed a spectrum analysis of the components but that because his spectrum analyzer was limited to 100 kilohertz, he would not have been able to observe any parasitic oscillation in the modules even had they been present. In his interview, he did state that during the initial testing using an oscilloscope, he saw noise on the peaks of the wave form.

During the Fort Totten investigation, investigators were able to obtain the components from Rosslyn and have them tested at WMATA's Carmen Turner facility in Landover, Maryland. On August 3, 2009, the Rosslyn modules were tested and found to have parasitic oscillation between the transmitter module and the receiver module similar to that found at Fort Totten. At the NTSB's request, WMATA reviewed historical occupancy data for Rosslyn track circuit C2-111. Although the track circuit was placed in service in 1977, historical data were available dating back to only October 1988 and were not comprehensive. The data showed that from October 1988 onward, track circuit C2-111 intermittently lost train detection and indicated "vacant" when trains were occupying the circuit. Track circuit C2-111 had always been equipped with GRS impedance bonds and GRS track circuit modules.

ATC Maintenance, Test, and Inspection Procedures

Manufacturer-Specified Maintenance for GRS Track Circuit Modules

Manufacturer-provided guidance for maintenance of the GRS track circuit modules used by WMATA specified quarterly maintenance testing to verify the stability of the frequency, modulation, and power level of the track circuit transmitter and the passband response and sensitivity level of the track circuit receiver. According to that guidance, once per quarter, the following are to be checked:

- The transmit power levels for the two TWC signals used to communicate train number, destination, length, and door status between the carborne system and the wayside. (The maintenance schedule calls for making root mean square [RMS] voltage measurements and recording the results on the track circuit module data sheet. If these levels are found to be "radically"[63] different from previous readings, the procedure calls for adjustments to be made to the module.)

- The transmit power level for the train occupancy detection signal used to sense the presence of a train within the boundaries of the track circuit. (The maintenance schedule calls for making an RMS voltage measurement and recording the result on the track circuit module data sheet. If this level is found to be "radically" different from previous readings, the procedure calls for an adjustment to be made to the module.)

- The transmit carrier frequencies[64] of both the track circuit and the TWC signals. (The maintenance schedule calls for making a frequency measurement and recording the result on the track circuit module data sheet. If the frequencies are found to be outside of the tolerances specified in the procedure, the defective subsystem is to be replaced.)

- The transmit modulation frequency[65] (code-rate) of the train occupancy detection signal. (The maintenance schedule calls for making a frequency measurement and

---

[63] The word "radically" is an undefined term used in the manufacturer's guidance.

[64] The *carrier frequency* is the main frequency used to carry signal energy from the transmitter to the receiver. This will be a sinusoidal waveform of constant frequency and peak-to-peak amplitude in the case of an unmodulated signal. Eight carrier frequencies are available for track circuit train occupancy detection: 2100, 2320, 2580, 2820, 3100, 3370, 3660, and 3900 hertz. Speed communications are carried out on one of two frequencies: 4550 or 5525 hertz.

[65] The *modulation frequency* is that frequency by which the much higher frequency carrier signal is modified in order to convey information. In the case of the WMATA track occupancy system, modulation is accomplished using

recording the result on the track circuit module data sheet. If the frequency is found to be outside of the tolerances specified in the procedure, the defective subsystem is to be replaced.)

- The center frequency and passband characteristics of the track circuit receiver input filter. (The maintenance schedule calls for making a voltage measurement with a known signal input at the center frequency of the receiver passband. Additional voltage level measurements are required with known signal inputs at frequencies above and below the center frequency in order to characterize the passband of the filter. All results are to be recorded on the track circuit module data sheet. If any of the filter characteristics are found to be outside of the tolerances specified in the procedure,[66] the defective subsystem is to be replaced.)

- The receiver sensitivity level for the train occupancy detection signal. (The maintenance schedule calls for making several peak-to-peak voltage measurements using an oscilloscope and recording the result on the track circuit module datasheet. If the levels are found to be "radically" different from previous readings, the procedure calls for the module to be adjusted.)

WMATA Track Circuit Maintenance Activities

WMATA has written instructions for employees responsible for maintaining, testing, and inspecting components of the Metrorail ATC system. Preventive maintenance instruction (PMI) 11000, "High Frequency Track Circuits," dated February 24, 1982, outlines the requirements for ATP track circuit adjustments. PMI 11000 states "3.3.4 Verify that a .06 ohm shunt ten (10) feet inside the transmit end of the track circuit will drop the track relay."

Another document, WMATA's *ATC System Integrity Maintenance Practices*, dated March 25, 2003, includes sections on track circuit adjustment and verification. Regarding track circuit verification, the guidance states the following:

10.4 **Verification:** Track circuits must be verified immediately after any adjustment, repair, or replacement of their vital components including: module, printed circuit boards, relay, resistors, coupling units, wires, cables, bonds, track transmitter loop, special track work or rails; and at least every three months. The verification test is described under the section titled "Safety Certification Tests."

---

a 50 percent duty cycle square-wave signal with a period varying from 333 milliseconds to 46 milliseconds. This modulation scheme is referred to as the code-rate, based on the six distinct modulation frequencies (code-rates) permitted in the design: 3.9, 4.6, 6.83, 10.1, 15.3, and 21.5 hertz.

[66] The procedure specifies attenuation at the center frequency to be less than 50 percent. Passband attenuation is required to be greater than 50 percent over the center frequency level for signals with frequency beyond about ±55 hertz from center frequency.

The "Safety Certification Tests" section of the guidance states, in part:

5.5   Track Circuit Verification Tests: Whenever components of a track circuit (including track-work) are replaced or adjusted a functional test of the track circuit must verify that the track relay will drop away when a soft shunt (.06 [ohm]) is installed between the running rails of the track. For double rail track circuits the test shunt should be installed ten feet inside the transmitter end.

The June 19, 2005, engineering bulletin and ATC safety notice issued after the Rosslyn incident added a requirement for a shunt placement in the middle of the track circuit when track circuits were being verified. The October 6, 2006, WMATA Metrorail engineering bulletin stated that after the installation of a US&S impedance bond in a GRS ATP track circuit, a verification shunt test should be performed using a 0.06-ohm shunt placed at three positions on the affected track circuits (at each end and in the middle).

At the time of the Fort Totten accident, WMATA had two draft ATC technical procedures that had not been approved by the Metrorail ATC assistant chief engineer, the Office of Engineering Support Services, and the TSSM assistant general superintendent. One of the draft documents—ATC technical procedure T181, *Track Circuit Adjustments*—was dated October 29, 2008. The procedures are used when adjusting track circuits equipped with either GRS or US&S modules. After the adjustments were made, the track circuits were to be verified in accordance with the procedures outlined in PMI T111, *Track Circuit Quarterly Shunt Test*. PMI T111, dated December 23, 2008, was also in draft form and had not been implemented at the time of the accident. The draft PMI T111 instructed that, for an audio frequency track circuit, a 0.06-ohm shunt should be placed (1) 10 feet inside the transmitter end of the circuit, (2) halfway between the transmitter and the receiver, and (3) 10 feet inside the receiver end of the circuit. The track circuit is verified when all three placements cause the track circuit relay to drop. As a remedial action in case the track circuit fails the validation test, the draft procedure stated, "if the track circuit fails the shunt test, protect train movement. Perform Procedure T181 and adjust or repair the track circuit immediately and repeat the shunt test."

In postaccident interviews, the CIT crew leader responsible for the installation of the new transmitter impedance bond on June 16 and 17, 2009, stated that PMI track circuit verification required that only one shunt be placed 10 feet inside the transmitter end of the circuit. But she said that when an impedance bond was replaced, her preference was to shunt in three places on the track circuit. The installer's supervisor said that he had seen her use two shunts when verifying a track circuit after a US&S bond installation but was not aware that she had ever used three.

The CIT supervisor said that, because of a lack of written procedures for installing the bonds, he had developed instructions himself and provided them to the crews installing US&S impedance bonds. The instructions included a section on track circuit adjustment that referenced the PMI 11000 track circuit verification procedures (placement of a single shunt 10 feet inside the transmitter end) for GRS track circuit modules.

The Red Line ATC mechanics who conducted verification tests on track circuit B2-304 the day after the impedance bond was replaced told investigators that they used the PMI 11000 procedures for GRS modules. They said they had no specific procedures for adjusting track circuits when US&S impedance bonds were installed with GRS track circuit modules.

During postaccident interviews, neither the installation crew leader nor the ATC mechanics mentioned the June 19, 2005, engineering bulletin and ATC safety notice stating that track circuits should be tested at the middle of the track circuit in addition to the transmitter end because of the possibility that a circuit could shunt at either end and fail to shunt in the middle. Nor did any of the ATC technicians indicate that they were aware of the October 6, 2006, engineering bulletin requiring three shunt placements. The document they did mention was PMI 11000. The TSSM CIT supervisor said he was aware of an engineering bulletin but understood that it applied only to high-current substation return impedance bonds and not to regular impedance bonds. None of the technicians interviewed were new hires; their service with WMATA Metrorail ranged from 6 to 23 years, with an average of 15 years' service.

At the public hearing on this accident, the WMATA superintendent of communications was asked about the process by which engineering bulletins such as the October 6, 2006, bulletin would have been distributed to ATC technicians. He stated that the procedure was for such bulletins to be distributed to each individual work center and then to each ATC employee. A sheet for each bulletin was used to document that each employee had acknowledged receipt of the bulletin. This sheet was to be retained for 2 years.

With specific reference to the October 6, 2006, bulletin, he said the following:

> I would say that, based upon information that has come to light since the June 22 accident, I believe that the distribution of the bulletins back in the 2005–2006 time frame was probably uneven. In other words, there were technicians who had that knowledge; there were other technicians who did not. Unfortunately, with only 2-year retention of the records, I was unable to verify that everyone had, in fact, signed off on acknowledging those bulletins.

WMATA uses form PM-1, *Track Circuit Adjustment*, to record all track circuit adjustments and verifications performed under the PMI 11000 procedure. Column 7 of the form is labeled "Shunt Test" and provides two check boxes to indicate whether a shunt was placed at the transmitter and/or the receiver end of the track circuit. The form does not include a place for indicating placement of a shunt at a third location. According to a WMATA representative, the draft T111 procedure, which is intended to replace the PMI 11000 procedure, includes a data sheet with columns to indicate placement of up to eight verification shunts depending on track configuration.

Current WMATA-Specified Maintenance for GRS Track Circuit Modules

Current WMATA guidance for track circuit maintenance is documented in three technical procedures: T111–*Track Circuit Quarterly Shunt Test*, T181–*Track Circuit Adjustments*, and T163–*GRS ATP Module Parasitic Oscillation Test*. At the public hearing for this accident, the former WMATA ATC assistant chief engineer stated that six additional track circuit tests would be added to the WMATA track circuit routine maintenance schedule: (1) a measurement of signal strength when a track is being verified, (2) a test for a received waveform signature indicative of the presence of corrugated rail, (3) an open bond line test to ensure that track circuit transmitter signal level is not high enough to cause a false vacancy indication on a downstream track circuit, (4) a periodic test for parasitic oscillation, (5) a test for excess distortion of the transmitted audio track circuit signal, and (6) a verification that the input signal to the track circuit receiver does not exceed the manufacturer's recommended maximum power level.

Under procedure T111, track circuits are to undergo a shunt test quarterly or whenever a change has been made that affects the operation of the track circuit. This procedure requires that a 0.06-ohm shunt be applied across the track and that the associated track circuit relay be observed. If the relay drops, the test is passed. If the relay fails to drop, the T181 procedure is to be followed.

The T181 procedure is to be performed whenever a change has been made that affects the operation of the track circuit. The T181 procedure—instituted on June 22, 2009, as a planned update of the PMI-11000 high-frequency track circuits maintenance procedure—outlines a series of tests designed to ensure that the associated track circuit relay will drop when the track circuit is shunted with a 0.06-ohm shunt. Two of the tests specified in the T181 procedure are relevant for the GRS track circuit modules used by WMATA. The first test calls for verification and adjustment of the direct current bias setting for the transmitter power output transistors. This test involves two direct current measurements. The second test calls for the verification and adjustment of the track circuit detection signal level. The procedure refers to the GRS *Operations and Maintenance Manual-Wayside Equipment* or the Alstom *Field Maintainer's Manual 5004B* (as appropriate) for a detailed description of the procedure to be followed. This test involves a shunt verification test according to PMI-111, measurement and recording of track circuit data according to PMI T121 (*Track Circuit Detection Signal Annual Test*), and verification by oscilloscope that the transmit and receive signals are free of distortion.

The T163 test is to be performed whenever a change is made that affects the operation of the track circuit, or as directed. The T163 procedure was instituted on August 9, 2009, in response to findings from the investigation of the Fort Totten accident. This test calls for the use of a 100-megahertz oscilloscope to observe the details of the output signal from the track circuit transmitter. Recorded data include oscillation type, frequency, amplitude, source frequency, source track circuit name, and receiver input signal level with a hard shunt in place. Three distinct types of oscillations are documented in the test procedure: one continuous and two described as "pulse-type." If type 4 oscillation (spurious signals that can compromise the fail-safe design of the track circuit) is detected, the signal level must be measured. Corrective action is to be taken if the level of the spurious signal exceeds 400 millivolts peak to peak.

Use of US&S Impedance Bonds with GRS Track Circuit Modules

The Metrorail track circuit replacement program procedures developed and implemented by WMATA involved the installation of US&S impedance bonds by WMATA crews, followed later by installation of US&S track circuit modules by Ansaldo contract crews. For that period of time between the installation of the new bonds and the installation of the new track circuit modules, the track circuits would be operated with US&S impedance bonds and GRS modules.

The WMATA ATC systems engineer told investigators that he had been involved in the track circuit replacement program from the development of the specifications for the track circuit replacement project through the approval of the products, review of the technical documentation, and final installation. Through bench testing, he identified an approximate 10-percent difference in resistive impedance between the US&S and GRS impedance bonds. He also stated that he connected a GRS module to a US&S impedance bond and monitored the output using different voltage ranges. He said he found no significant deviation from what would be expected from a circuit using all GRS components. He further stated that track circuits using components from different manufacturers were tested at three locations in rail yards to confirm that no incompatibilities existed that would affect reliability.

The systems engineer told investigators that the contract called for all track circuit modules to undergo safety certification tests before installation. These tests were carried out by WMATA ATC technicians. All impedance bonds were required to be tested by US&S before they were shipped to WMATA. In addition, the contract required US&S to submit a hazard mode and effect analysis for WMATA's approval. According to the systems engineer, US&S had provided WMATA with all the required documentation specified in the contract.

The first track circuit replacements were at three sites on the Orange Line. The ATC systems engineer stated that the installations at these three locations did not indicate any problems.

The October 6, 2006, engineering bulletin indicated that WMATA had consulted with technical representatives from both manufacturers (Ansaldo for the US&S bonds and Alstom for the GRS modules) about using the US&S and GRS components together. The ATC systems engineer said that he discussed the matter with the Alstom manager of train detection products who indicated that, because he had no knowledge of impedance bonds from other manufacturers, he could not recommend using GRS and non-GRS components together. The systems engineer said he did not recall specific discussions about the issue with Ansaldo representatives.

At the public hearing on this accident, the site safety officer for Alstom said that his company, through a September 7, 2004, letter, subject: "Impacts of the Use of Non OEM [original equipment manufacturer] Components," had advised all of its customers not to use Alstom components with components from other manufacturers. The letter cited an investigation of a freight car derailment that had determined that "the root cause of the failure(s) lay with a defect or design inconsistency of a product sub-assembly provided by a supplier other than Alstom." The letter further stated the following:

Alstom believes that the use of third party components, in the absence of rigorous industry design and safety standards, presents, not only a customer quality issue, but also constitutes a serious and increasing risk to overall signaling system safety. [Emphasis in the original.]

The letter also stated,

While one product line [switch machines] has been highlighted [in this letter], this is a much bigger issue as it relates to rework and maintenance of train control systems and the constituent components of all vital products: relays, signals, interlockings, track circuits, etc.

The Alstom manager of train detection products told investigators that he had asked that the reference to track circuits be included in the letter because of WMATA's plan to install US&S impedance bonds with GRS track circuit modules.

The WMATA ATC assistant chief engineer was included on the 19-page distribution list attached to the letter, but he could not recall whether he had ever received it. Both the Alstom manager of train detection products and the WMATA ATC systems engineer stated that the 2004 Alstom letter was not mentioned during their discussions about using track circuit components made by different manufacturers.

ATC technicians who had performed the preventive maintenance inspection in the accident area the day after the new impedance bond was installed for track circuit B2-304 raised concerns about the compatibility of components. One of the technicians stated,

We have no adjustment procedures for adjusting these bonds with a GRS module and a US&S bond. There has been a long history of problems every time CIT puts one of these bonds in. Generally, we have speed command problems because ... there's an impedance mismatch that's pretty commonly known throughout the railroad. You talk to any technician on the railroad, when CIT comes and puts these bonds in, they know they're in for problems. Again, there's no adjustment procedures for these things.

The WMATA ATC systems engineer stated that he was aware of some ATC technicians' concerns about combining equipment from different manufacturers. He stated that these concerns generally revolved around the need to change transmitter power settings during track circuit adjustments after a new bond was installed. He said that he was told that the track circuits were being verified using three shunts and that, if the track circuit verified using the three shunts, he did not consider the power level change to be an issue because of the small difference in the impedance between the two bonds. He stated that he issued the October 6, 2006, engineering bulletin to ensure that the track circuits using components from different manufacturers were verified using three shunts.

According to the WMATA ATC systems engineer, currently about 26 Metrorail track circuits are using US&S high-current impedance bonds with GRS track circuit modules.[67] No loss-of-shunt problems have been identified with any of those circuits.

Postaccident Inspection of Maintenance Communication Components

Each of the racks in a train control room and at wayside ATC installations has a telephone jack that connects to a maintenance communication system that allows workers in train control rooms to communicate with personnel at other train control rooms or equipment locations. The system is a deenergized two-wire network configured for handheld telephones. Maintenance personnel or others who must access the right-of-way can plug a handheld telephone into a wayside telephone jack and communicate with someone using another telephone plugged into a jack in the train control room.

The telephone lines are routed from the train control room to the field and linked in series to telephone jacks in every track junction box. The track junction boxes are also used to terminate the train control room bond cables and the cable connection from the track circuit impedance bonds.

Postaccident inspection of several track junction boxes between Fort Totten and Takoma found many of the telephone jacks inoperative because of broken terminals or disconnected wiring. The inoperative telephone jacks were either missing or found unsecured inside the track junction boxes. Track junction boxes with missing telephone jacks also had exposed mounting holes. Some of the telephone jacks that were found disconnected inside track junction boxes had bare wire terminals lying loose inside the box. Several bare wire terminals were in proximity to track circuit impedance bond terminal connections.

Vehicle Data Recorders

The cars making up train 112 at the time of the accident were 1000-series cars, which are the oldest cars in the Metrorail fleet. None of these cars had vehicle data recorders or any other recording devices.

The cars making up train 214 at the time of the accident were four 3000-series cars in the lead followed by two 5000-series cars. Train 214 was equipped with three onboard event recorders[68] (one onboard recorder per each paired set of cars) and six data acquisition modules (DAM) (one on each car); all nine recording devices were available for downloading train data.

---

[67] These were circuits in which impedance bonds had been replaced as part of WMATA's traction power upgrade program.

[68] WMATA uses the term "Federal Railroad Administration (FRA) recorder" to describe this recording system; however, to avoid confusion with the Federal Railroad Administration, a U.S. government agency, this report will refer to this system as the "onboard event recorder" or the "onboard recorder."

As stated above, each paired set of cars from train 214 had an onboard recorder. The onboard recorder was a microprocessor-based, memory-based hardened module that recorded train data provided by the vehicle monitoring system (VMS) central unit. The train data recorded included data from each major train system: propulsion; brakes; ATC; doors; heating, ventilating, and air conditioning (HVAC); and auxiliary power supply. However, only the onboard recorder in the lead paired set of cars recorded ATC data such as regulated speed and limited speed.

In addition to the onboard recorders, each car had a DAM. The DAM recorded analog and digital data from its car's train system (for example, doors, brakes, HVAC, auxiliary power supply), and it recorded train speed and distance covered. The DAM sends its car's data to the VMS central unit for monitoring and, in turn, the DAM data are recorded by the onboard recorder.

The three onboard recorders from train 214 were downloaded; however, only the last paired set of cars (5066/5067) had accident data. The onboard recorders from the first and second paired set of cars (3036/3037 and 3256/3257) had stopped recording before the accident. Because the onboard recorder from the lead paired set of cars stopped recording before the accident, no ATC information was available for analysis.

Of the six available DAMs from train 214, only the DAMs from cars 3036, 3256, and 3257 had accident data. The DAM data from car 3037 failed to download, and the DAM data from cars 5066 and 5067 had stopped recording before the accident.

Out of the nine available recording devices from train 214 (three onboard recorders and six DAMs), only one onboard recorder and three DAMs had accident data. Based on the downloaded data, train 214 had been stopped for about 49 seconds when the collision occurred. As a result of the collision, train 214 moved ahead about 10 feet.

Tests and Research

Sight-Distance Testing

On July 18, 2009, investigators conducted sight-distance tests in the accident area. The tests were conducted at the same time of day as the accident under similar weather conditions. The two trains used for the tests were of the same configuration as the accident trains and used the same type of equipment.

The simulated struck train was positioned in the right-hand curve on track B2 at the same location as train 214 on the day of the accident. The second train, simulating the striking train, was used to determine at what point the rear of train 214 would have been visible to the operator of train 112.

The tests revealed that the train 112 operator would have had a partial view of the rear of the stopped train from about 1,180 feet away. A full view of the rear of train 214, including both red marker lights, would not have been available to the operator of train 112 until the trains were 470 feet apart.

Speed and Braking Calculations

Because of the absence of event data recorders on train 112, investigators did not have speed and braking information for the striking train. However, the train control system did record the time the train entered and left each track segment. Train 112 was being operated in automatic mode at the time of the accident. Using WMATA-supplied train braking and acceleration data as well as known train response to speed inputs from the signal system, the NTSB was able to develop a computer program to simulate the position and speed of train 112 up to the point that manual braking had been applied. As a speed target, the simulation used the speed commands from the signal system based on the train's position on the various track segments and the time elapsed on these segments. Acceleration or braking was applied as necessary. The simulation then integrated these accelerations to determine a new speed and integrated that speed to determine a new position for the next time step. The signal system had recorded the time the train entered and left each signal circuit segment, and the simulation matched those times.

Because the exact time of the collision was uncertain, an actual braking profile could not be developed. The NTSB therefore simulated several braking scenarios by entering various emergency braking locations into the simulation program. The decelerations taken from the emergency braking schedule table provided by WMATA were adjusted for the track slope for the location of the accident.[69] Use of a collision time that was early in the range of possible times for the collision produced a terminal speed for train 112 that best matched the collision speed of 49 mph that was calculated based on damage to the railcars.

On the day of the accident, recorded train control system data indicated that at 4:56:41 train 112 began to receive a 0 mph speed command while the train was in block B2-336. While the train slowed and stopped, the train moved into block B2-328 while the 0 mph speed command continued. Based on calculated speed and position history and assuming normal service braking, train 112 would have come to a stop about 4:57:03. According to the recorded signal data, about 17 seconds later, at 4:57:20, the ATC system changed the speed commands transmitted to train 112 from 0 mph back to 55 mph, which would have caused the train to begin to accelerate to that speed automatically even though train 214 remained stopped ahead.

Although the emergency brake was found in the activated position, the operator's reaction time could not be determined. The position and speed calculations indicated that, had the train 112 operator immediately applied the train's emergency brakes (by depressing the emergency brake mushroom) when the rear of train 214 was fully visible (when the trains were separated by 470 feet), the train would not have been able to stop and would have struck the rear

---

[69] WMATA also provided track geometry data.

of train 214 while traveling about 24 mph. Activation of emergency braking 3 seconds after train 214 had become fully visible would have resulted in train 112 striking train 214 while traveling about 44 mph.

Insulation Resistance Testing

Following the accident, investigators asked WMATA representatives to provide copies of maintenance records that included results of insulation resistance tests. The representatives responded that no insulation resistance testing had been conducted.

The Metrorail ATC technical procedure T031 *Cable Insulation Resistance Testing*, dated November 25, 2008, requires the periodic testing of all cables installed in conduits, in ducts, along tunnel walls, or buried along the right-of-way, and of all wires and cables entering and leaving train control rooms, equipment cases, and junction boxes. The cables and wires must be tested for insulation resistance from each conductor to all other conductors in the cable or wire and from each conductor to ground. Insulation resistance for conductors used in a power source of less than 600 volts must exceed 1 megaohm. Resistance in wires and cables used in a power source greater than 600 volts must exceed 10 megaohms. The tests must be conducted every 10 years or after any new installations. At the time of the accident, the T031 procedure was new, it was not superseding another procedure, and it was still undergoing review before final approval.

Investigators performed postaccident insulation resistance tests on bond cables and telephone lines installed from the Fort Totten train control room to both main tracks in the vicinity of the two impedance bonds for track circuit B2-304. The cables were routed together from the train control room to the field locations through conduits and manholes along an underground duct bank between the two main tracks. For several days before the accident, the Washington, D.C., area experienced heavy rains. Following the accident, the manholes were found partially filled with water, and the bond cables and telephone lines were submerged. After several days of dry weather, the bond cables were tested and found to have insulation resistance of less than 500 kiloohms to ground. As a result of the postaccident insulation resistance tests, the absolute block on track B2 through the accident area (which had been implemented after the accident) was extended to track B1 between Fort Totten and Takoma.

Investigators used a spectrum analyzer to test for stray audio frequencies from outside sources that could possibly affect the track circuits. Harmonics from the 720-hertz traction power return frequency and the adjacent track circuit frequency were detected on the bond cables for track circuit B2-304. Identified harmonics of adjacent track circuit frequencies were also found on the bond cables, but at very low levels that did not pass through the track circuit module receiver filter.

Postaccident testing revealed that maintenance communication telephone lines were faulted to ground inside the track junction boxes along the wayside. The insides of the track junction boxes were heavily rusted, and the wire terminals were grounded to the metal case of the track junction boxes through the rust. A spectrum analyzer detected the frequency for track circuit B2-304 on the communication lines, but the signal was determined to be of insufficient strength to be recognized as a valid signal by the track circuit module receiver.

Corrugated Rail

The investigation identified corrugated rail as a condition that can possibly lead to track circuit failure. Rail-head corrugations can cause or intensify electrical arcing between the train wheels and the rail, and this arcing can create harmonics that have been shown to effectively mimic a valid track circuit signal that can be accepted by the receiver via the normal signal path. For such harmonics to lead to a track-circuit failure, trains must be traveling at a certain speed, and the corrugations on the rail must occur at certain intervals. Because these signals only occur when a train is moving and they cease to be generated when a train is stopped, WMATA ATC engineers considered the harmonics caused by corrugated rail to be benign.

Safety Oversight of Transit Operations

Federal Transit Administration

The Federal Transit Administration (FTA) is one of 11 operating administrations of the U.S. Department of Transportation (DOT). The purpose of the FTA, which the agency carries out largely through its grant program, is to help cities and communities across the country develop improved mass transportation systems. Unlike other DOT modal administrations, such as the FRA, the FTA does not have the statutory authority to promulgate or enforce safety regulations or to regulate the operations of transit agencies. The agency does have limited regulatory authority in the areas of drug and alcohol use and state safety oversight, but it does not have authority for direct enforcement of these regulations.

Over the years, the NTSB has issued several recommendations to the FTA and its predecessor agency, the Urban Mass Transportation Administration, addressing the need for those agencies to promulgate regulations and to establish mandatory safety guidelines for any transit agency that receives federal funding. In response, the FTA has maintained that transit agency compliance with FTA guidelines and recommended best practices cannot be made a condition of federal financial assistance. The extent of the FTA's efforts thus far has been to encourage transit agencies to adhere to industry best practices and to NTSB recommendations.

State Safety Oversight Agencies

In 1991, the NTSB made safety recommendations to the FTA regarding the need for state oversight of rail transit system safety. In response, Congress authorized the FTA to develop a rule creating a state-managed safety and security oversight program for rail transit agencies not regulated by the FRA. This regulation, *Rail Fixed Guideway Systems; State Safety Oversight*, was originally issued on December 27, 1996, as Title 49 CFR Part 659, with the requirements of the regulation going into effect 1 year later.

Part 659 requires that each state with an existing or anticipated rail system subject to the requirements of the regulation designate a state agency, other than the transit agency itself, to provide safety oversight. In locations where a rail system operates in more than one state, as does the WMATA Metrorail system, each of the affected states may designate its own oversight agency, or the states may collectively designate a single agency to act for all in implementing the requirements in the regulation. Currently, 27 separate state safety oversight programs have been implemented across the United States. Some oversight agencies, such as the California Public Utilities Commission and the Massachusetts Department of Public Utilities, have the authority to promulgate and enforce safety regulations. Others, such as the Tri-State Oversight Committee (discussed below), do not have regulatory authority.

Although the designation of the oversight agency is subject to review by the FTA, the agency cannot disapprove a state's designated oversight agency or specific individuals assigned to it. The FTA also does not specify any minimum educational or technical qualifications for individuals performing the oversight function.

Tri-State Oversight Committee

The state safety oversight agency for WMATA Metrorail[70] is the Tri-State Oversight Committee (TOC), which was established in 1997 by a memorandum of understanding (MOU) between the Virginia Department of Rail and Public Transportation and the departments of transportation of Maryland and the District of Columbia. The MOU specifies that TOC comprise six representatives, two from each of the aforementioned agencies. The secretary of transportation for the state of Virginia, the secretary of transportation for the state of Maryland, and the director of transportation for the District of Columbia select their respective members. The MOU does not address either the appropriate qualifications for members of TOC or the length of their terms of service. The MOU specifies that TOC members must select a chair and a vice chair who serve in those capacities for 1 year. At the end of the 1-year term, the vice chair becomes the chair, and a new vice chair is selected by the TOC members. The MOU also permits each agency to designate an alternate representative.

Before the June 22, 2009, accident at Fort Totten, TOC met once each quarter to conduct business. Subsequent to the accident, the committee has met at least monthly. TOC has no physical office location; the members share the facilities of the agencies they represent. Online information about TOC has been enhanced since the Fort Totten accident, and can be viewed at <http://www.tristateoversight.org>.

Of the six TOC members, only one, representing Virginia, is assigned to work full time for TOC. The current TOC chair, a part-time TOC member, estimated that before the Fort Totten

---

[70] References to WMATA from this point forward mean the WMATA Metrorail system.

accident he devoted about 30 percent of his time to TOC activities. He said that since the accident he has devoted 80 to 90 percent of his time to WMATA oversight. In calendar year 2009, TOC members collectively worked 6,670 hours on oversight responsibilities.

The MOU establishing TOC defines a quorum required for decision-making as one representative from each agency. A majority vote is required to take any official action. TOC members have the authority to make routine decisions regarding the application of TOC program standards and procedures; however, any changes to this document require approval of the senior leadership of the members' employing agencies.

TOC cannot establish or enforce standards of performance for WMATA with respect to safety-critical areas of performance such as operations, equipment, track, signal, hours of service, and equipment crashworthiness. TOC also lacks the authority to compel WMATA to comply with its own rules, standards, and procedures, or to take significant action should WMATA fail to comply with an element of its system safety program plan.[71]

In performing its oversight responsibilities, TOC's primary activities include annually reviewing and approving WMATA's system safety program plan, including any changes to the plan. TOC also requires WMATA to conduct safety reviews and to submit the findings to TOC for review. Through use of a third-party contractor, TOC also conducts on-site safety reviews every 3 years to determine whether WMATA's safety practices and procedures are in compliance with the system safety program plan. Any areas that are identified as those in need of corrective action are incorporated into a corrective action plan (CAP).

As of February 3, 2010, a total of 48 CAPs from previous triennial audits were still classified as open, that is, unresolved. This included 9 CAPs from events in 2004, 6 from 2005, 6 from 2006, 11 from 2007, and 13 from 2008. Of the 48 open CAPs, 2 were related to the Rosslyn incident in 2005 (discussed elsewhere in this report), and 15 were related to NTSB recommendations issued in connection with WMATA accidents occurring at the Woodley Park-Zoo/Adams Morgan (Woodley Park) station in 2004,[72] at the Dupont Circle[73] and Eisenhower Avenue[74] stations in 2006, and at the Mt. Vernon Square station in 2007.[75] TOC lacks the authority to compel WMATA to complete the requirements specified in the CAPs.

---

[71] When a state's program standard is approved by the FTA, each rail agency must develop and implement a written system safety program plan that complies both with 49 CFR Part 659 and with the oversight agency's program standard. The oversight agency must review and approve the system safety program plan.

[72] *Collision Between Two Washington Metropolitan Area Transit Authority Trains at the Woodley Park-Zoo/Adams Morgan Station in Washington, D.C., November 3, 2004*, Railroad Accident Report NTSB/RAR-06/01 (Washington, DC: National Transportation Safety Board, 2006).

[73] *Washington Metropolitan Area Transit Authority Train Strikes Wayside Worker Near Dupont Circle Station, Washington, D.C., May 14, 2006*, Railroad Accident Brief NTSB/RAB-08/01 (Washington, DC: National Transportation Safety Board, 2008).

[74] *Washington Metropolitan Area Transit Authority Train Strikes Wayside Workers Near Eisenhower Avenue Station, Alexandria, Virginia, November 30, 2006*, Railroad Accident Brief NTSB/RAB-08/02 (Washington, DC: National Transportation Safety Board, 2008).

Before the Fort Totten accident, TOC members were not permitted on WMATA property to perform their field oversight responsibilities without the permission of WMATA. Since the accident, WMATA has implemented procedures to allow TOC access to WMATA properties to perform oversight activities.

WMATA Board of Directors

At the time of the accident, WMATA was governed by a board of six directors, two from each of the three jurisdictions. For Virginia, the directors are appointed by the Northern Virginia Transportation Commission; for the District of Columbia, by the Council of the District of Columbia; and for Maryland, by the Washington Suburban Transit Commission. In the case of Virginia and Maryland, the directors are members of their respective commissions. Directors serve at the pleasure of their appointing authorities.

During the public hearing for this accident, the chairman of WMATA's Board of Directors was asked about the role of the Board. He stated that the job of WMATA's board was to

> establish the broad policy and the broad direction to set goals for the general manager and for the agency and to respond to any indications that those broad goals are not being accomplished.

When asked whether the general manager normally briefed the Board of Directors on the number of open corrective action items from previous investigations or audits or any other activity that would generate a recommendation or finding, the chairman of WMATA's Board of Directors responded as follows:

> Not on a routine basis. We count on the general manager and his staff to identify for us issues that require our attention and we don't second guess them on that.

The WMATA Board chairman was also questioned during the public hearing about the safety indicators tracked by WMATA. One of the hearing exhibits[76] was a copy of a presentation to the WMATA Board of Directors on June 25, 2009, from the WMATA Customer Services, Operations, and Safety Committee that included the statement, "Metro continues to influence a positive safety culture by taking immediate actions to correct recognized hazards." Examples of safety indicators in the presentation included station and parking lot injuries, escalator injuries, derailments, smoke and fire events, and improper door operations.[77] The presentation did not

---

[75] *Derailment of Washington Metropolitan Area Transit Authority Train Near the Mt. Vernon Square Station, Washington, D.C., January 7, 2007*, Railroad Accident Report NTSB/RAR-07/03 (Washington, DC: National Transportation Safety Board, 2007).

[76] NTSB Public Hearing Exhibit P1-O, *WMATA Safety and Security Report 6-25-2009*.

[77] After expanding 8-car train service on the Orange, Red, and Green lines, WMATA experienced several instances of doors opening with the rear cars not properly aligned with the station platform due to operators stopping 8-car trains at the 6-car position rather than the end of the platform.

address progress on TOC safety audit findings, open CAPs, or FTA and NTSB recommendations. The WMATA system safety program plan requires that the WMATA general manager regularly provide this information to the Board of Directors to help them carry out their responsibility for system safety oversight.[78]

Safety Oversight Within WMATA

The individual within WMATA with primary responsibility for managing and overseeing the agency's safety program is the chief safety officer. The chief safety officer oversees all safety operations, interacts with all departments within WMATA regarding safety, and provides safety-related information to the WMATA general manager and the Board of Directors.

During the investigation of the January 6, 1996, Metrorail train collision at the Shady Grove station,[79] the NTSB noted that WMATA employees reported a perceived lack of communication and a sense of information isolation within the organization. These concerns were addressed at the time by an internal WMATA safety review committee, which recommended to the WMATA Board of Directors that WMATA change its organizational structure to have the safety department report directly to the general manager. This internal safety committee recommendation was subsequently adopted and implemented.

However, following the November 3, 2004, collision between two WMATA trains at Woodley Park station,[80] WMATA restructured its organization to again remove the direct reporting relationship between the safety department and the general manager. In its report on the Woodley Park accident investigation, the NTSB stated its concern that the reorganization of the safety department could "... recreate the systemic information isolation that existed within WMATA prior to the Shady Grove accident, which in turn could inhibit serious safety problems from being identified or adequately addressed." In response to that concern, the NTSB issued the following safety recommendation to the FTA:

> Assess the adequacy of the Washington Metropolitan Area Transit Authority's current organizational structure and ensure that it effectively identifies and addresses safety issues. (R-06-4)

In response to FTA and NTSB concerns, WMATA revised its organizational structure again in May 2006 so that the chief safety officer reported directly to the general manager. Based on this change, the NTSB classified Safety Recommendation R-06-4 "Closed—Acceptable Action" on October 5, 2007.

---

[78] *System Safety Program Plan*, Washington Metropolitan Area Transit Authority (Washington, DC: Washington Metropolitan Area Transit Authority, 2008), p. 30.

[79] *Collision of Washington Metropolitan Area Transit Authority Train T-111 With Standing Train at Shady Grove Passenger Station, Gaithersburg, Maryland, January 6, 1996,* Railroad Accident Report NTSB/RAR-96/04 (Washington, DC: National Transportation Safety Board, 1996).

[80] NTSB/RAR-06/01.

According to information provided by WMATA representatives at the public hearing on the Fort Totten accident, during the past 5 years, the chief safety officer has reported variously to WMATA's auditor general, its general manager, its assistant general manager for safety and security, and, at the time of the accident, WMATA's chief administrative officer. In July 2009, reporting channels were changed so that the chief safety officer would report directly to the WMATA general manager. In November 2009, the chief of the Metro Police became the acting chief safety officer reporting directly to the WMATA general manager.

According to information gathered during this accident investigation, TOC members had, for several years before the accident, expressed concern to WMATA regarding the safety department's position within the organization. Most recently, an October 2008 letter from TOC to the WMATA general manager reiterated its position that there should be a direct reporting relationship between the safety department and the general manager. TOC asked the general manager to reestablish direct reporting, expressing concern that the general manager would otherwise not be able to adequately support his responsibilities under WMATA's system safety program plan.

FTA Audit of TOC and WMATA

The FTA's Office of Safety and Security conducts periodic audits of state safety oversight agencies to evaluate their compliance with requirements of 49 CFR Part 659.

The 2005 FTA audit of TOC focused on the ability of TOC to develop and implement plans and procedures required for the implementation of 49 CFR Part 659. As a result of this audit, the FTA issued nine deficiency findings and one recommendation regarding TOC's implementation of 49 CFR Part 659 requirements. Over the next 2 years, TOC and WMATA were unable to close several of these audit findings, prompting the FTA to conduct a series of meetings with TOC and WMATA executive leadership about WMATA's ability to identify, elevate, and address safety deficiencies within its own agency as well as WMATA's lack of responsiveness to TOC.

In December 2009, the FTA conducted another audit of TOC and WMATA. This audit was originally scheduled for mid-2010 but was accelerated at the request of the DOT secretary and a member of Congress. For this audit, the FTA departed from its normal process of focusing primarily on the state safety oversight agency. According to the FTA,

> In the aftermath of (1) the Ft. Totten collision and (2) in light of the well-publicized difficulties that TOC encountered assessing WMATA's right-of-way safety program, FTA decided to assess WMATA's safety program as well. WMATA's acting Chief Safety Officer also requested that FTA's audit more closely examine WMATA's system safety program.

The 2009 audit focused primarily on three areas:

- The effectiveness of both TOC's and WMATA's implementation of the FTA's state safety oversight rule.

- The level and quality of coordination between TOC and WMATA to ensure safety for WMATA's passengers and employees.

- Followup on three open noncompliance findings from the FTA's 2007 audit of TOC.

The audit team identified deficiencies specific to TOC's implementation of the state safety oversight regulation and its oversight of WMATA. The final audit report[81] listed 11 findings directed to TOC and 10 recommendations directed to WMATA.[82]

The FTA reported that it had issued findings to TOC in which it had determined that a required component of TOC's program did not meet the FTA's state safety oversight program requirements. Regarding WMATA, the FTA "issued recommendations where FTA believes improvement is needed."

With regard to hazard identification and communication, the FTA audit report states the following:

> WMATA does not have a process, including a single point of responsibility, which ensures the timely identification and analysis of hazards. As mentioned previously, WMATA's Executive Leadership Team and Safety Department personnel were unable to provide a comprehensive matrix or assessment that identified the agency's on-going evaluation and management of its most serious safety hazards and concerns. Upon questioning, several different WMATA managers indicated that these issues had been identified already in the accidents that were being investigated at WMATA. This WMATA approach is reactive and prevents getting value from the proactive aspects of the hazard management process.

The FTA audit report also states the following:

> Based on discussions and record reviews at WMATA's Track Structures and System Maintenance, it does not appear that there is effective interdepartmental coordination regarding the identification and management of maintenance-related safety hazards between Rail Operations Delivery, Rail Transportation, Track Structures and Systems Maintenance, Vehicle Engineering, the Infrastructure Renewal Project Group, and Engineering Services. Further, through interviews and records reviews, FTA determined that there is no formal process for identifying and managing the likely safety impacts of budgetary decisions affecting maintenance.

---

[81] *State Safety Oversight Program: Audit of the Tri-State Oversight Committee and the Washington Metropolitan Area Transit Authority, Final Audit Report* (Washington, DC: U.S. Department of Transportation, Federal Transit Administration, 2010).

[82] See appendix C of this report for a complete listing of all 21 findings and recommendations.

In general, FTA auditors identified a lack of resources dedicated to the safety department within WMATA, a lack of stability within the safety department, and a general lack of attention from senior management. In his March 4, 2010, speech regarding FTA's audit of WMATA and TOC, the FTA administrator stated the following:

> [WMATA's] safety department has been isolated both from top management and from other [WMATA] departments. In fact, the Safety Department has had their access and authority questioned by other operating departments. And this dynamic has seriously undermined the Safety Department's ability to conduct its safety responsibilities.[83]

In the March 4 speech, the FTA administrator also stated that

> [The] FTA found evidence that WMATA's Safety Department is not "plugged-in" to critical conversations, decision-making meetings and reporting systems that provide information on hazards and potential safety concerns throughout the agency. Key documents, reports, and decisions are not consistently shared with the Safety Department. In addition, the Safety Department does not receive and review available monthly reports from the Rail Operation, Quality, or Maintenance departments. On numerous occasions during the audit interviews, <u>Safety Department representatives indicated that they were learning for the first time that information of a safety nature was being documented by operating departments.</u> [Emphasis in the original.]

The administrator went on to note that, at the time of the FTA audit, the WMATA safety department had a 25-percent vacancy rate, that the department had been reorganized six times since 2005, and that WMATA had had four chief safety officers since 2007.

Five of the FTA's 10 audit recommendations to WMATA addressed safety department deficiencies. These recommendations may be summarized as follows: The FTA believes WMATA should (1) determine the resources and expertise necessary for the safety department and staff the department accordingly, (2) ensure that safety department staff has access to all operations and maintenance information so that potential safety risks can be identified, (3) require that safety-related information be made available to all departments, and (4) develop and implement a process to ensure that the chief safety officer can communicate safety priorities to the general manager in a consistent and timely manner.

Because the FTA lacks direct regulatory authority over rail transit agencies, WMATA is under no legal obligation to address these recommendations.

---

[83] P. M. Rogoff, "Oral Statement on Federal Transit Administration's recent audit of WMATA and the Tri-State Oversight Committee," speech read to the National Capital Region Delegation of the United States Congress, March 4, 2010, Washington, D.C.

Current Legislative Action

On December 7, 2009, the DOT secretary submitted draft legislation to the Congress that, if enacted, would provide the FTA with a significant increase in its ability to provide oversight of the rail transit system. The proposed Public Transportation Safety Program Act of 2009 is intended to accomplish three key objectives:

- Authorize the DOT secretary to establish and enforce federal safety standards for rail transit systems that receive federal transit assistance.

- Allow states eligible for federal transit assistance to hire and train state oversight personnel to enforce new federal regulations.

- Require the state agencies conducting oversight to be fully financially independent from the transit systems they oversee. The FTA would enforce all federal regulations where states choose not to participate in the program or where the state program is found to lack the necessary enforcement tools.

Other Information

Previously Issued Safety Recommendations

In addition to urgent Safety Recommendation R-09-15 (discussed elsewhere in this report), the NTSB issued several other safety recommendations while the investigation of this accident was still ongoing.

On July 13, 2009, the NTSB issued the following safety recommendation to WMATA:

Take action to enhance the safety redundancy of your train control system by evaluating track occupancy data on a real-time basis in order to detect losses in track occupancy and automatically generate alerts. Alerts should prompt actions that include immediately stopping train movements or implementing appropriate speed restrictions to prevent collisions. (R-09-6 Urgent)

In a September 9, 2009, letter, WMATA responded that because no commercial systems currently available could provide the Metrorail system with the kind of alerts that the NTSB has recommended, the agency has taken steps to develop such a system. This includes expanded use of the loss-of-shunt tool. The letter stated that after the accident, WMATA began reviewing the loss-of-shunt information twice per day. Further, WMATA was working with commercial vendors to fully develop the system. Based on this response, on December 30, 2009, the NTSB classified Safety Recommendation R-09-6 "Open—Acceptable Response." (For more information about expanded use of the loss-of-shunt tool, see the section below, "Safety Actions Taken by WMATA Since the Accident.") At the public hearing on this accident, WMATA representatives stated that the agency is also working with vendors and developers on a real-time train detection system as well as methods of providing system redundancy.

On July 13, 2009, the NTSB issued the following safety recommendation to the FTA:

Advise all rail transit operators that have train control systems capable of monitoring train movements to determine whether their systems have adequate safety redundancy if losses in train detection occur. If a system is susceptible to single point failures, urge and verify that corrective action is taken to add redundancy by evaluating track occupancy data on a real-time basis to automatically generate alerts and speed restrictions to prevent train collisions. (R-09-7 Urgent)

The FTA responded that on July 13, 2009, within hours after the urgent recommendation was issued, it had circulated a "Dear Colleague" letter to all rail transit operators to disseminate the information in the recommendation. The letter was also posted on the FTA's website the following day. The letter also indicated that the FTA is requesting that transit agencies provide information about specific train control systems and about compensating systems the agency may be able to develop should it determine that a single-point failure could occur. The FTA stated that it had held discussions with the transit industry regarding Safety Recommendation R-09-7 at its Safety and Security Roundtable Meeting in Portland, Oregon, in July 2009 and continues to work with the American Public Transportation Association (APTA) to review APTA's role in private consensus standard setting and in ensuring effective communication with the transit industry.

The NTSB subsequently learned that the FTA had hired a consultant to (1) inventory rail transit systems to identify train control systems in use today and collect data, (2) identify redundant systems in place and monitor technology currently available, and (3) determine agency responses to Safety Recommendation R-09-7. The consultant's report is expected to serve as a clearinghouse for information regarding best practices for addressing safety. The FTA has also been discussing Safety Recommendation R-09-7 with transit agencies to determine agency compliance. Pending a further update on FTA activities, on December 30, 2009, the NTSB classified Safety Recommendation R-09-7 "Open—Acceptable Response."

In a February 16, 2010, letter regarding Safety Recommendation R-09-7, the FTA informed the NTSB that, in September 2009, the agency had hosted the 13th annual Rail Transit State Safety Oversight Program Meeting in Tempe, Arizona. The meeting was attended by 88 representatives from rail transit agencies, state oversight agencies, the FTA, and industry. NTSB representatives also attended the meeting to provide insight and answer industry questions about Safety Recommendation R-09-7 as well as Safety Recommendations R-09-17, -18, and -19 (discussed below). On October 21, 2009, the FTA issued a letter to state safety oversight program managers requesting their assistance in following up with the rail transit agencies in their jurisdictions to confirm and monitor the actions being taken to address the issues identified in the NTSB recommendations.

Also on September 22, 2009, the NTSB made the following safety recommendations to the FTA:

> Advise all rail transit operators that use audio frequency track circuits in their train control systems that postaccident testing following the June 22, 2009, collision between two rail transit trains near the Fort Totten station in Washington, D.C., identified that a spurious signal generated in a track circuit module transmitter by parasitic oscillation propagated from the transmitter through a metal rack to an adjacent track circuit module receiver, and through a shared power source, thus establishing an unintended signal path. The spurious signal mimicked a valid track circuit signal, bypassed the rails, and was sensed by the module receiver so that the ability of the track circuit to detect the train was lost. (R-09-17 Urgent)

> Advise all rail transit operators that use audio frequency track circuits in their train control systems to examine track circuits that may be susceptible to parasitic oscillation and spurious signals capable of exploiting unintended signal paths and eliminate those adverse conditions that could affect the safe performance of their train control systems. This work should be conducted in coordination with their signal and train control equipment manufacturers. (R-09-18 Urgent)

> Advise all rail transit operators that use audio frequency track circuits in their train control systems to develop a program to periodically determine that electronic components in their train control systems are performing within design tolerances. (R-09-19)

The FTA made its initial response to the safety recommendations in a November 6, 2009, letter to the NTSB. Regarding urgent Safety Recommendations R-09-17 and -18, the FTA stated that it had, on the day the recommendations were made, issued a "Dear Colleague" letter advising rail transit agencies of the NTSB's recommendations and urging them to examine their track circuits and remove conditions that could create unintended paths for spurious signals. Based on this response, on April 27, 2010, the NTSB classified Safety Recommendations R-09-17 and -18 "Closed—Acceptable Action."

Concerning Safety Recommendation R-09-19, the FTA responded that it plans to provide additional guidance for the development of a periodic testing program as described in the recommendation. Based on this response, on April 27, 2010, the NTSB classified Safety Recommendation R-09-19 "Open—Acceptable Response."

Also on September 22, 2009, which was the same day that the NTSB issued urgent Safety Recommendation R-09-15 (discussed elsewhere in this report) to WMATA, the NTSB issued the following recommendation to WMATA:

Develop a program to periodically determine that electronic components in your train control system are performing within design tolerances. (R-09-16)

WMATA initially responded to Safety Recommendations R-09-15 and -16 in an October 23, 2009, letter to the NTSB. Urgent Safety Recommendation R-09-15 asked that WMATA examine Metrorail track circuits that may be susceptible to parasitic oscillation and spurious signals and eliminate conditions that could affect the safe performance of the Metrorail train control system. WMATA responded that since early August 2009, WMATA Engineering and Support Services staff had been examining track circuits found to have timing issues. Through this process, WMATA ATC technicians identified and replaced four track circuit modules that exhibited symptoms similar to the failure mode at Fort Totten.

In response to Safety Recommendation R-09-16, WMATA indicated that it had added six additional circuit tests to its periodic testing procedures. At the public hearing on this accident, the former WMATA ATC assistant chief engineer described these additional tests as follows: (1) a test that will measure signal strength when a track is being verified; (2) a test for a signal signature indicating the presence of corrugated rail, which can cause loss-of-shunt indications; (3) an open bond line test to ensure that track circuits have not increased transmitter amplitude to the point that they cause a false vacancy indication on another track circuit; (4) a periodic test for parasitic oscillation; (5) a test for distortion on the audio frequency signal going out of the module; and (6) a verification that the input signal to the track circuit receiver does not exceed the manufacturer's recommended maximum. The former WMATA ATC assistant chief engineer said that a warning is also being added to the track circuit verification test procedures indicating that a bobbing track circuit cannot be verified until the source of the bobbing has been identified and corrected. Based on these responses, on April 27, 2010, the NTSB classified Safety Recommendations R-09-15 and -16 "Open—Acceptable Response."

In a June 11, 2010, letter to the NTSB, WMATA provided an update of its activities in response to Safety Recommendations R-09-15 and -16. WMATA informed the NTSB that, with regard to Safety Recommendation R-09-15, the WMATA Office of Engineering and Support Services had completed testing all track circuits using "components of the type identified as problematic in the Fort Totten investigation." The letter stated that, while the examination had not identified any track circuits exhibiting parasitic oscillation other than the four reported previously (in the October 23, 2009, response letter), WMATA had identified and replaced an additional four sets of bonds and modules that, while they did not exhibit parasitic oscillation, did produce test results that WMATA considered to be unsatisfactory.

With regard to Safety Recommendation R-09-16, the June 11, 2010, letter stated that WMATA had created a new protocol for train control equipment testing. The referenced protocol is the T163 procedure previously discussed in this report. The letter included a copy of the T163 procedure. The "Introduction" section of the T163 procedure states, in part, "Either all or portions or a variation of this procedure will be incorporated into the future periodic maintenance program."

On September 22, 2009, the NTSB also issued the following safety recommendation to Alstom:

> Assist the Washington Metropolitan Area Transit Authority, and other rail transit operators and railroads that use your audio frequency track circuit equipment, in examining their train control systems for susceptibility to parasitic oscillation and spurious signals capable of exploiting unintended signal paths, and implementing measures to eliminate those adverse conditions that could affect the safe performance of their train control systems. (R-09-23 Urgent)

On October 20, 2009, Alstom responded that it was performing ongoing tests in its own laboratories, on WMATA property, and at other sites and that its engineers were working with NTSB investigators to further test the modules used for the Metrorail system. Alstom subsequently demonstrated possible methods of mitigating the parasitic oscillation in WMATA's GRS ATP track circuit modules. One method involved the use of insulating blocks to separate the transistor heat sinks from the module, thus interrupting the unintended path of the parasitic oscillation. Another method involved installing ferrite chokes[84] on the power amplifier leads to the modules. Pending the results of Alstom's implementation of these measures and a demonstration of their effectiveness, on April 27, 2010, the NTSB classified Safety Recommendation R-09-23 "Open—Acceptable Response."

On June 26, 2010, Alstom informed the NTSB[85] that it had recommended that WMATA[86] install ferrite beads (chokes) on the power amplifier leads of all Generation 2 GRS modules remaining in service "while other techniques are being evaluated and tested." The letter accompanying the June 26 e-mail stated that Alstom "is in the process of developing three specific methods of mitigation in addition to the method already recommended to WMATA," each of which involves modifying the design of a power amplifier circuit board. The letter also stated that Alstom had conducted on-site testing at other transit properties known to use GRS Generation 2 audio frequency track circuit modules[87] and that the limited sample of track circuits tested at each location showed "no evidence of the type of conditions reported at WMATA." The letter went on to state that, subsequent to this preliminary testing at other transit sites,

> Alstom has developed a detailed test procedure and purchased new test equipment in order to conduct testing of all remaining modules at these customer locations. Alstom is in the process of arranging site visits to all of its customers using Generation 2 modules to test and document the condition of all of the identified track circuits. This information

---

[84] *Ferrite chokes* reduce radio-frequency and electromagnetic interference.

[85] In an e-mail with an attached letter dated June 22, 2010, which provided an update on Alstom's mitigation testing activities.

[86] WMATA informed the NTSB on July 1, 2010, about a meeting it had with Alstom on June 7–8, 2010, in which Alstom orally recommended that WMATA install ferrite chokes on the power amplifier leads of all Generation 2 GRS modules in service as a temporary measure to mitigate parasitic oscillation until Alstom provides a permanent solution. WMATA stated that it had not started installing the ferrite chokes and that it expected Alstom to provide an engineering change notice for the proposed installation.

[87] According to Alstom, the Generations 3 and 4 GRS modules represent significant design developments, and no evidence of pulse-type parasitic oscillations has been observed in those modules.

will identify any track circuits that are of concern and allow for temporary mitigation as required.

Attached to the letter was a copy of an Alstom procedure to collect power amplifier input signal data and receiver amplifier output signal data for track circuits equipped with Generation 2 GRS modules.

On September 22, 2009, the NTSB issued the following safety recommendations to the FRA:

Advise all railroads that use audio frequency track circuits in their train control systems that postaccident testing following the June 22, 2009, collision between two rail transit trains near the Fort Totten station in Washington, D.C., identified that a spurious signal generated in a track circuit module transmitter by parasitic oscillation propagated from the transmitter through a metal rack to an adjacent track circuit module receiver, and through a shared power source, thus establishing an unintended signal path. The spurious signal mimicked a valid track circuit signal, bypassed the rails, and was sensed by the module receiver so that the ability of the track circuit to detect the train was lost. (R-09-20 Urgent)

Require all railroads that use audio frequency track circuits in their train control systems to examine track circuits that may be susceptible to parasitic oscillation and spurious signals capable of exploiting unintended signal paths and eliminate those adverse conditions that could affect the safe performance of their train control systems. This work should be conducted in coordination with their signal and train control equipment manufacturers. (R-09-21 Urgent)

Require all railroads that use audio frequency track circuits in their train control systems to develop a program to periodically determine that electronic components in their train control systems are performing within design tolerances. (R-09-22)

On October 22, 2009, the FRA informed the NTSB that it had surveyed all FRA-regulated railroads to determine their possible use of audio frequency track circuits for train detection and that the railroads were all aware of the WMATA accident and the subsequent safety recommendations. The FRA also indicated that it would contact the railroads that use audio frequency track circuits to determine what measures each railroad has taken or will take to eliminate possible failures in the circuits and to continuously monitor track circuit performance. Based on this response, on May 18, 2010, the NTSB classified Safety Recommendation R-09-20 "Closed—Acceptable Action." Also on May 18, 2010, Safety Recommendations R-09-21 and -22 were classified "Open—Acceptable Response." On July 22, 2010, the FRA gave the NTSB a spreadsheet with the results of its survey, which indicated that no FRA-regulated carriers use audio frequency track circuits for train detection in their train control systems.

Development of Improved Loss-of-Shunt Tool

After the accident, WMATA implemented twice-per-day use of the loss-of-shunt tool to analyze loss-of-shunt events experienced by the 3,000 track circuits across the Metrorail system. The loss-of-shunt tool has been programmed to automatically generate a daily report covering all Metrorail operations. Each morning and evening WMATA engineers review the loss-of-shunt reports for the previous 24-hour period. These reviews are conducted 7 days per week. Under the new procedures, a WMATA engineer, within 2 hours of receiving the report, will review the information and notify the appropriate office of the review findings. Activities in response to the findings are posted on WMATA's website.[88]

WMATA has reported that, with the support of the provider of the current AIM software, it is developing a system designed to provide real-time alerts for loss-of-shunt events. The first step, according to WMATA, is the development of an improved loss-of-shunt detection algorithm that has a lower false-alarm rate. The new logic being developed will

- Include interlockings in the analysis (not present in the current tool).
- Ignore the ghost trains created by false occupancies.
- Include train length information (received in TWC data at every platform).
- Include track circuit length information.
- Include maximum acceleration rates (both positive and negative) for the train.

This new algorithm fits the known train length into known track-circuit boundaries, allowing the system to generate graphic displays that show track-circuit occupancies in dimensions of distance and time. This information is displayed to scale so that an engineer can readily recognize a false report of train occupancy.

In November 2009, WMATA initiated experimental development work for an automated loss-of-shunt warning system. Loss-of-shunt events detected using the 3-second-rule algorithm are detected within minutes of their occurrence. This information is reported using the new graphical format discussed above and forwarded via e-mail to an on-call ATC engineer. Both the old and new loss-of-shunt tool algorithms are implemented on an independent computer using the AIM data collected from the wayside. Once development of the algorithm is completed, WMATA will determine whether to migrate the programming to the AIM computer or to local processors at the wayside, or both. WMATA reports that it is considering using the alarm output from the new loss-of-shunt tool to disable speed commands to a zone of track circuits; however, this would require extensive design, installation, and test work.

---

[88] For a list of completed track circuit maintenance, see
<http://www.wmata.com/about_metro/track_circuit_archive.cfm>.

Event Recorders on WMATA Metrorail Trains

As the result of its investigation of two WMATA Metrorail accidents, one in 1982[89] and the other in 1996,[90] the NTSB made the following safety recommendations to WMATA:

Maintain the carborne[[91]] monitors on existing Metrorail cars and require their installation on cars presently on order. Acquire the necessary equipment to read the monitor tapes. (R-82-74)

Finalize the specifications for a new advanced-technology carborne monitoring system and, once that is complete, retrofit existing Metrorail cars with monitors/recorders during rehabilitation and require that all new Metrorail cars be equipped with devices. (R-96-39)

In response to these recommendations, WMATA began installing onboard recorders in newly acquired cars and established a program to retrofit existing cars with onboard recording devices. In 2002, WMATA stated that the 5000-series cars were equipped with onboard recorders, that the 2000- and 3000-series cars would be retrofitted by 2005, and that the 4000-series cars were expected to be equipped by 2014. WMATA reported that it was unsuccessful in testing the installation of onboard recorders in the 1000-series cars. WMATA stated that after 2014, which is the anticipated completion date of installing onboard recorders in the 4000-series cars, the 1000-series cars would be reevaluated to determine if advances in technology would enable the installation of onboard recording devices. At that time, WMATA also stated that the 1000-series cars were scheduled for retirement between 2012 and 2015. The NTSB classified Safety Recommendations R-82-74 and R-96-39 "Closed—Acceptable Action" on June 10, 1991, and May 28, 2002, respectively.

Currently, WMATA revenue trains are configured with three or four married-pair car sets of two passenger cars. Each paired set of cars (except for the 1000 and 4000 series) has a hardened memory module incorporated into the overall VMS. The hardened memory module portion of the VMS records train variables (ATC information, speed, distance, door status, brakes, emergency stop, and so on) and is referred to as the onboard recorder. Only the onboard recorder in the lead set of cars records ATC information (for example, regulated speed and limited speed). The number of onboard recorders on a particular train is based on the number of sets of cars (excluding any 1000- and 4000-series cars). For example, a 6-car train could have a maximum of three onboard recorders.

Since December 2006, the NTSB has investigated five WMATA accidents after which investigators downloaded data from onboard recorders from 3000-, 5000-, and 6000-series cars.

---

[89] *Derailment of Washington Metropolitan Area Transit Authority Train No. 410 at Smithsonian Interlocking, January 13, 1982,* Railroad Accident Report NTSB/RAR-82/06 (Washington, DC: National Transportation Safety Board, 1982).

[90] NTSB/RAR-96/04.

[91] At the time these recommendations were issued, the term *carborne* was used to designate onboard recorders.

The NTSB was able to successfully recover accident data from 6 of 11 installed onboard recorders, including 2 of the 5 recorders installed on lead cars. In three of the five accident investigations, no recorded ATC information was successfully downloaded.

WMATA provided the NTSB with documentation on the reliability performance analysis of the VMS from April 2006 through March 2010. These data showed 737 VMS failures that would have prevented the recording of train data on the onboard recorders. Currently, WMATA does not have a formal program to monitor the reliability of the onboard recorders.

Federal Requirements for Event Recorders on Trains

FRA regulations at Title 49 CFR 229.135 require that railroad locomotives (but not transit trains) be equipped with crash-survivable event recorders capable of recording, at a minimum, the following eight parameters:

- Train speed

- Selected direction of motion

- Time

- Distance

- Throttle position

- Applications and operations of the independent brake

- Applications and operations of the dynamic brake, if so equipped

- Cab signal aspect(s), if so equipped and in use

WMATA is a transit agency that is not subject to FRA regulations. Not all rail transportation systems are governed by the FRA's regulations. The FRA governs the operation of standard gage railroads that are part of the general railroad system of transportation such as freight, intercity passenger, and commuter railroads. Except under some very limited and clearly defined circumstances,[92] the FRA does not regulate any rapid transit operations (for example, WMATA Metrorail) in urban areas that are not connected with the general railroad system.

Within a 2-month period in 2001, the Chicago Transit Authority (CTA) experienced two similar rear-end collisions involving CTA rapid transit trains. In its report,[93] the NTSB addressed the safety issue of the adequacy of event recorders on rail transit vehicles and issued the following safety recommendation to the FTA:

---

[92] See appendix A to Title 49 CFR Part 209, "Statement of Agency Policy Concerning Enforcement of the Federal Railroad Safety Laws."

[93] *Two Rear-End Collisions Involving Chicago Transit Authority Rapid Transit Trains at Chicago, Illinois, June 17 and August 3, 2001,* Special Investigation Report NTSB/SIR-02/01 (Washington, DC: National Transportation Safety Board, 2002).

Require that new or rehabilitated vehicles funded by Federal Transit Administration grants be equipped with event recorders meeting Institute of Electrical and Electronics Engineers Standard 1482.1 for rail transit vehicle event recorders. (R-02-19)

The FTA, in its response, stated that it does not have the authority to mandate onboard event recorders. On August 29, 2008, the NTSB classified this recommendation "Closed—Unacceptable Action."

WMATA Emergency Preparedness

Training. WMATA trains emergency responders at its facility in Landover, Maryland. The facility includes a tunnel that replicates an actual Metrorail tunnel. The tunnel has track with a simulated third rail, an emergency access catwalk, standpipes, an emergency trip station box,[94] an emergency tunnel evacuation cart,[95] and two railcars that were damaged in a previous accident. According to WMATA, since opening in May 2002, the facility has trained more than 14,000 emergency responders.

In May 2006, a passenger rail vehicle emergency evacuation simulator was added to the facility. The simulator, which was developed by the FRA, is a New Jersey Transit commuter railcar that can be rotated up to 180 degrees to simulate different railcar positions after an accident.

WMATA offers three levels of training for emergency responders and employees: awareness level, operations level, and command level. The awareness level is a 1-day course that includes general information about the rail system, the right-of-way, railcars, and safety. The operations level is a 2-day course that expands on the topics presented in the awareness course. The command level is an additional 2-day course for emergency responders who could serve as incident commander at a rail incident. Topics in the training include emergency response maps, standpipes, the ventilation system, emergency evacuation carts, emergency trip stations, and use of a WSAD.

Drills. On July 19, 2009, WMATA and local emergency responders held a readiness exercise at the West Falls Church Yard in Falls Church, Virginia. The drill simulated a train malfunction and subsequent collision. The goals of the drill were to conduct a hands-on exercise to test the responders' ability to mitigate a fire and medical event and to work with WMATA personnel and safety equipment and procedures.

---

[94] The *emergency trip station box* has an emergency button to stop third-rail power, a schematic drawing that shows the length of track on which power will be removed, and a telephone to contact the OCC.

[95] The *emergency tunnel evacuation cart* is designed to move along the rails and can be used to bring patients out of, or emergency equipment into, the tunnel.

Procedures. WMATA and the Metropolitan Council of Governments developed the "Metrorail and Fire/Rescue Services Emergency Procedures Policy Agreement," dated May 13, 1997. The agreement lists procedures for responding to emergencies in and around the rail system. The agreement includes procedures for incident notification, emergency response, and command and control.

Previous NTSB Study of WMATA Metrorail

The NTSB first addressed the safety of the WMATA Metrorail system in 1970, when it conducted a special study of the proposed system while it was still under construction. That study did not constitute a complete technical review of the entire system but rather offered observations on the various identifiable hazards within the proposed system. Examples of hazards discussed in the report include station design, separation of tracks, and train car design. The report resulted in one recommendation to WMATA:

> Develop the capability within your organization for system safety engineering and apply system safety principles to all aspects of the proposed metro system to identify, assess, and correct those deficiencies identified by the analysis. (R-70-18)[96]

In advocating the system safety engineering approach to analyzing the proposed Metrorail system, the NTSB cited Military Standard MIL-STD-882,[97] which outlines a formal approach to identifying and mitigating safety hazards through engineering, design, education, and supervisory control practices. Although not widely applied to transit systems at the time, the system safety approach the NTSB recommended to WMATA in 1970 was eventually required of all rail transit agencies' system safety program plans under 49 CFR 659.31. MIL-STD-882 is also now cited in the FTA implementation guidelines for 49 CFR Part 659[98] and is incorporated in the hazard management process of WMATA's current system safety program plan. The FTA issued the state safety oversight regulation on December 27, 1995.

WMATA Metrorail Fault Tree Analysis

In June 1980, the firm of De Leuw, Cather, & Company performed a fault tree analysis[99] for WMATA to identify events that could lead to train collisions during revenue service. The

---

[96] This safety recommendation was classified "Closed—Acceptable Action" on November 17, 1975.

[97] See <http://safetycenter.navy.mil/instructions/osh/milstd882d.pdf>.

[98] Information obtained from the FTA's website: <http://transit-safety.fta.dot.gov/publications/sso/Imp_Guidelines/pdf/Imp_Guidelines.pdf>.

[99] A *fault tree* represents all conceivable causes of a specified system failure in terms of failures in the underlying subsystems and critical components. A *quantitative analysis* attaches probabilities to the various component and subsystem failures so that a critical path calculation can be made to identify the most likely chain of events resulting in a particular system failure. A *qualitative analysis* generates the same fault tree, only without the probabilities. The WMATA-sanctioned study represented a qualitative analysis.

analysis did not evaluate possible failure modes involving components of the train control system.

Safety Actions Taken by WMATA Since the Accident

Since the accident, WMATA has taken steps to improve the identification, analysis, and communication of safety issues within its operations. In addition to developing an improved loss-of-shunt tool and expanding the use of that tool, WMATA is working with a contractor to develop a real-time train operations monitoring system as recommended by the NTSB in its urgent Safety Recommendation R-09-6, previously cited.

WMATA has also changed its personnel and organizational structure to increase the size and expertise of its safety staff. In a May 14, 2010, letter to TOC, the interim general manager of WMATA described several recent changes in the WMATA organization. Recent staff changes include hiring a new chief safety officer, who reports directly to the general manager. An assistant chief safety officer is also being hired to provide additional management of the safety department and Metrorail operations. WMATA has also filled six new positions in the safety department and plans to fill six additional vacancies in the department. The new positions will be responsible for investigating incidents and accidents, analyzing safety trends, reviewing and documenting safety policies and procedures, and ensuring adherence to safety protocols.

Safety officers have been assigned to each Metrorail division to improve communication between front-line staff in the operating division and the safety department. WMATA has also established a Safety Action Team that includes representation from the various departments within the organization, with the goal of improving the communication of safety-related information to all employees. As part of the effort to improve communication throughout the organization, WMATA is developing a safety management system that combines its various disparate systems for tracking information such as passenger injuries, employee human resources, and equipment maintenance. In that new system, reports are consolidated into a single repository for review and tracking. The system is being tested in WMATA bus operations and is tentatively planned to be expanded to the rest of WMATA operations in the late summer or fall of 2010.

Finally, WMATA has collaborated with the DOT Transportation Safety Institute to expand its training program for safety department staff and other vital personnel. According to the general manager of WMATA, Metrorail personnel are receiving additional training in rail system safety, incident investigation, and emergency management.

Analysis

Exclusions

The weather at the time of the accident was clear and dry, and the accident occurred in daylight. Sight-distance tests conducted at the same time of day and under the same weather conditions as on the day of the accident revealed no influences of weather or visibility that would have contributed to the accident.

The investigation revealed that the operators of both train 112 and train 214 were qualified to perform their duties. Examination of the work/rest histories based on time sheets provided by WMATA showed that both operators worked split shifts. Although research has indicated that split shifts, and shift work in general, can result in fatigue and related physiological problems, no evidence was found to suggest that either operator was suffering the effects of fatigue before or at the time of the accident. The operator of train 112 had been off duty for almost 15 hours before reporting for duty on the day of the accident and had been on duty for just over 1 hour when the collision occurred. At that time, the operator of train 214 had been on duty for less than 2 hours since returning to duty after his mid-day break.

Postaccident toxicological tests for both train operators were negative for the presence of alcohol and illegal drugs. The investigation also found no evidence of a medical condition on the part of either train operator that would have affected their ability to perform their jobs safely.

Postaccident visual examination of the track in the accident area found nothing remarkable with regard to track geometry. Postaccident measurements for gage, cross-level, alignment, and rail side wear were all within WMATA standards. Track in the accident area had been inspected by two Metrorail track inspectors who had walked the track 2 days before the accident. They noted no track defects. A review of track inspection reports for the 6 months prior to the accident revealed nothing remarkable for the accident track.

The rails on the Metrorail system are ultrasonically inspected five times per year. The last inspection before the accident was conducted on March 18, 2009. No rail defects were detected in the area of the collision during that inspection. On July 23, 2009, an ultrasonic inspection of the B2 track between the Takoma and Fort Totten stations found no indications of a potential rail failure or an undetected rail crack that could contribute to a signal failure. Rail-head profile measurements showed minimal wear, and no corrugations were visible. None of the inspection records or track conditions revealed a history of preexisting track problems within the area of the collision.

The NTSB conducted a detailed examination of the postaccident mechanical condition of the cars from both trains. The examination revealed that the brakes on both trains were applied at the time of the collision and that the brakes had been working properly. Polishing and wear patterns on the braking components in every instance were what would be anticipated in a fully functioning system. Analysis of the dynamic interaction between the cars on the striking train determined that the brake rigging on that train was not binding, fouling, chafing, or dragging before the collision. Postaccident brake testing on the cars from the striking train that were not destroyed in the collision revealed that the brakes on each car met or exceeded the brake rate standards. The testing and inspections indicated that the braking system on train 112 would have decelerated and stopped the train according to the specified rates.

The investigation determined that five of the six cars on train 112 had deferred maintenance items, with several related to the braking system. Maintenance had been deferred on these cars because of delays in obtaining the specialized replacement parts needed to make the repairs. Metrorail management had determined that the cars could continue in service until the parts arrived, and the investigation confirmed that the cars' braking systems performed normally on the day of the accident.

The NTSB therefore concludes that the following were neither causal nor contributory to the accident: weather, training and qualifications of the train operators, fatigue, use of alcohol or illegal drugs by the train operators, track structure and rail integrity, and condition and performance of train mechanical equipment.

Accident Sequence

On the afternoon of the accident, the operator of train 112 was making her first inbound trip, following behind train 214, which was following train 110. Records show that when train 214 moved onto track circuit B2-312 (between the Takoma and Fort Totten stations) it was traveling about 49 mph. But just before train 214 moved from track circuit B2-312 onto track circuit B2-304, the ATC system changed its authorized speed from 55 to 45 mph[100] in order to slow the train and provide adequate separation between it and train 110 ahead. With train 214 occupying track circuits B2-312 and B2-304, the speed commands for following train 112 changed from 55 mph to 0 mph. This caused train 112 to immediately begin to decelerate and eventually stop.

As train 214 moved completely onto track circuit B2-304, the track circuit failed to detect its presence, as had occurred for almost every train that had preceded it for the previous 5 days. Because speed commands are only transmitted when a train is detected as occupying the track circuit, no speed commands were transmitted to train 214. By design, the system defaulted to 0 mph. The momentum of train 214 was insufficient to carry it either onto the next track circuit or onto a portion of track circuit B2-304 (near the transmitter end) where its presence might have been detected. The train therefore came to a stop with no "awareness" from the ATC system that it was there. Consequently, the ATC system transmitted speed commands to train 112 even though train 214 was stopped ahead.

---

[100] Speed commands are actually generated though the ATP and ATO subsystems of the ATC system, but for convenience in this analysis, the train control system elements and subsystems will be referred to generically as the ATC system unless specific features of a subsystem are discussed.

The NTSB concludes that the Metrorail ATC system stopped detecting the presence of train 214 (the struck train) in track circuit B2-304, which caused train 214 to stop and also allowed speed commands to be transmitted to train 112 (the striking train) until the collision.

Performance of Operator of Train 112

As shown by sight-distance testing, as train 112 began accelerating after its brief stop, the train operator would not have been able to see the rear of train 214 because of the curvature of the track and the fencing that separates the Metrorail tracks from the adjacent CSX tracks. She thus would have had no immediate indication that her train was not receiving the proper speed commands.

The emergency brake of train 112 was found in the activated position. The NTSB attempted to determine whether it was reasonable to expect the operator to apply emergency braking in time to prevent the collision as her train rapidly approached the rear of the stopped train. At the time of the accident, train 112 was being operated in automatic mode (ATO). This was the normal operating mode for Metrorail trains, and it was the operating mode for which the system was designed. According to Metrorail officials, all trains at the time should have been operating in ATO.[101]

Although the operator of train 112 had been working as a train operator for only a few months, she had regularly operated Red Line trains during rush hour. She thus would have been aware of the short headways between trains that often require speed changes and schedule adjustments to maintain train separation. She would likely, on a number of occasions, have had her train stopped by the ATC system because of trains ahead. She would thus likely have come to trust in the reliability of the system to operate trains safely with very little input from the train operator.

Trust is a fundamental element in human-automation interaction. When an automated system has proven to be accurate and reliable, operators are inclined to trust the automated system even over their own diagnosis. Research has also shown that operators are likely to fail to detect automation failures in highly dependable ("trusted") systems.[102]

According to a passenger on train 112, when the train stopped, the operator announced that the train was stopping because of a train ahead. But from that location, according to postaccident sight-distance testing, the operator could not have actually seen that there was a

---

[101] The operator of train 214 had elected to operate his train in manual mode.

[102] R. Parasuraman, R. Molloy, and I. Singh, "Performance Consequences of Automation-Induced Complacency," *The International Journal of Aviation Psychology*, vol. 3, no. 1 (1993), pp. 1–23. Also see N. Bagheri and G. A. Jamieson, "Considering Subjective Trust and Monitoring Behavior in Assessing Automation-Induced "Complacency," in *Proceedings of the Human Performance, Situation Awareness and Automation Conference*. (Marietta, GA: SA Technologies, 2004).

train ahead. She may simply have assumed the presence of the other train because of her experience. In other words, she may have assumed the ATC system was doing its job.

After a brief stop, the train's speed commands returned, and the train began to move. This also would have been consistent with the operator's expectation. She would have assumed that the train ahead had proceeded, thus permitting her to continue. Even once she saw the train ahead, she would have had no reason to act until she had time to recognize that the train ahead was stopped and that the automated system had failed to initiate braking of her train. Therefore, the NTSB concludes that even though the operator of train 112 activated emergency braking before the collision, there was not enough time, once train 214 came into full view, to stop the train and avoid a collision.

Performance of Operator of Train 214

On numerous occasions, the operator of train 214 had refused to operate his train in automatic mode, as required by WMATA, because of his concerns about the ability of the system to ensure proper station stops. The operator stated his belief that he was allowed to violate Metrorail operating procedures because train operators "have the ultimate and final responsibility for the safety of the passengers on their particular trains...." The intent of such a provision in the rules, which is common among railroads and transit agencies, is to allow operating employees to modify an operating rule or procedure only under unusual circumstances when complying with a rule or procedure would create a risk to safety. The operator did not provide any evidence to justify noncompliance with operating procedures regarding train operating modes.

In manual mode (Mode 2, Level 1), which the operator was using at the time of accident, the train operator controls acceleration and braking, but the maximum speed is still constrained by the ATC system. Thus, had the train operator not manually stopped his train when he lost speed commands, the ATC system would have intervened to apply the brakes. Therefore, the collision protection between adjacent trains normally provided by the ATC system is still enforced whether the trains are being operated in manual mode or in ATO. The ability of track circuit B2-304 to detect train 214 also would not have been different because the train was being operated in manual mode rather than in ATO. The NTSB concludes that the operator's decision to operate train 214 (the struck train) in manual mode during the evening rush hour period was in violation of Metrorail rules, but track circuit B2-304 was failing to detect trains, regardless of whether they were operating in manual or automatic mode.

Assuming that the train can fit within the length of the faulty track circuit, the possibility of stopping within the circuit is affected by the speed of the train as it enters the circuit. Trains operating at slower speeds require less stopping distance and therefore may be more likely to come to a stop within a faulty track circuit after receiving a 0 mph speed command in that circuit. Speed commands are based on the relative position of the trains regardless of whether a train is being operated in manual or in ATO. Therefore, the operating mode (manual or ATO) of a train ahead does not affect the speed commands received by any trains following it.

Recorded speed data from train 214's onboard event recorder show that the train was traveling much slower than the authorized speed commands it was receiving. The speed command given to the train just before it entered track circuit B2-304 was 45 mph. As train 214 entered the track circuit, it was traveling about 25 mph. The operator of train 214 said that there was congestion in the area, and he had been slowing at times for train 110 that was ahead of his train before the accident. It is not unusual to operate below the maximum authorized speed in manual mode when the operator anticipates that the train will likely have to stop soon. The operator stated that as train 214 entered the faulty track circuit, he attributed the 0 mph speed command to his proximity to the train ahead, and the NTSB believes that he would have had no reason to suspect that the train control system had malfunctioned. Slow train entry speeds would also have been possible any time there was congestion ahead of the faulty track circuit regardless of whether trains were operating in automatic or manual mode. The NTSB concludes that because train 214, which was being operated in manual mode, was traveling at a much slower speed than the authorized speed commands it was receiving, train 214 stopped completely within the faulty B2-304 track circuit when its detection was lost and it received a 0 mph speed command.

Performance of the OCC

The OCC was designed to monitor overall train operations, to tailor system operation in response to unusual traffic conditions, and to provide a recovery capability in the event of equipment failure or other unanticipated events. OCC controllers are able to see train movements on their display screens; however, this information is not, nor was it designed to be, sufficient or timely enough to allow controllers to provide warnings of imminent train collisions. OCC controllers can affect train movements at certain locations through the use of wayside signals and switches, but they must rely on the ATP subsystem to maintain separation between trains operating in revenue service.

In performing their respective functions, both the OCC and the ATP subsystem rely on accurate track occupancy information. The OCC AIM controller display is incapable of accurately tracking and displaying the instantaneous position of a train that is operating through an area with malfunctioning track circuits. The algorithm used by the ATP subsystem to compute the speed commands does not take into account information concerning the past status of track occupancies or speed commands, which makes the subsystem incapable of tracking train movements and limits its ability to recognize and appropriately respond to anomalies in track circuit occupancy detection.

The AIM display was designed to provide OCC controllers with the information they need to monitor traffic flow around the railway and to respond to events such as isolated equipment failures. The displays are not optimized, nor are they intended, for direct, individual, real-time train control. The fidelity of the information is dependent on the ability of the display to accurately update the information based on changes in wayside status. A review of the AIM controller display around the time and in the location of the Fort Totten accident indicated that, in areas where the wayside signaling system was functioning normally, the display consistently and accurately depicted changes in wayside occupancy data within about 1 second. Conversely, in areas where the signaling system was functioning abnormally, the AIM display failed to accurately depict the presence and location of trains.

WMATA had implemented OCC AIM computer algorithms to identify malfunctioning track circuits and alert the controller via alarms under certain conditions. The NTSB considered whether OCC controllers could have prevented this accident if they had acted on the multiple ARB and NRB alarms that occurred in the 5 days before the accident near Fort Totten. However, it is not clear what actions OCC controllers were required to take in response to these alarms, and the programmed behavior of the AIM software—returning a track circuit graphic display status icon to "normal" without requiring controller acknowledgment—masked the presence and severity of potential track circuit failures. Further, the extremely high incidence of track-circuit alarms (that is, about 5,000 ARB and 3,000 NRB alarms per week) would have thoroughly desensitized OCC controllers to the track circuit malfunctions occurring across the Metrorail system. Therefore, the NTSB concludes that, because of the design of the WMATA OCC information management system and the high number of track circuit failure alarms routinely generated by that system, OCC controllers could not have been expected to be aware of the impending collision or to warn either train operator.

Urgent Safety Recommendation R-09-6, issued by the NTSB to WMATA on July 13, 2009, recommended that WMATA evaluate "track occupancy data on a real-time basis in order to detect losses in track occupancy and automatically generate alerts." WMATA has reported that it is working with the provider of the current AIM software to develop a system designed to provide real-time alerts for loss-of-shunt events. The first step, according to WMATA, is to develop an improved loss-of-shunt detection algorithm that will reduce the false-alarm rate for reported track circuit failures. A reduced rate of suspect alarms, coupled with greater engineering attention to reported loss-of-shunt events, should allow OCC controllers to better monitor the operating conditions across the system and to respond more effectively to anomalies. The NTSB supports these efforts and will continue to monitor WMATA's progress toward meeting its goals.

Emergency Response

The operator of train 214 reported the collision to the OCC, giving the location as chain marker 311+00. The collision caused third-rail power to go down immediately on track B2 (the accident track); about 10 minutes after the report of the accident, the OCC controller deenergized third-rail power on track B1.

The first transit police officer arrived on the scene about 5 minutes after the collision. The first medic arrived within 10 minutes of the collision. The assistant chief of operations for District of Columbia Fire and Emergency Medical Services acted as the incident commander and established a unified command system with the responding agencies and the railroads. Mutual aid resources were requested and received from surrounding areas in Maryland and Virginia. During the course of the response, the incident commander established an evacuation group, a rescue and extrication group, and a medical group. The battalion chief in charge of the medical group estimated that all patients were treated and transported within about 90 minutes after the accident.

As a result of the collision, the rear car of train 214 telescoped into the first car of train 112, making the recovery of occupants from the lead car of the striking train a difficult and dangerous extrication operation that required extensive manpower, resources, and time. The NTSB concludes that considering the challenges of the recovery operations, the emergency response was well coordinated and effectively managed.

Loss of Train Detection in the ATC System

At the time of this accident, the ATC system was reporting track circuit B2-304 as vacant even while it was occupied by train 214. Based on that report, the system transmitted speed commands of 55 mph to train 112, which caused the train to automatically start and begin to accelerate to that speed. The ATC system transmitted speed commands of 55 mph to train 112 even as the train struck the rear of train 214.

The ATC system identifies a block of track (or track circuit) as being vacant or occupied based on the position (energized or deenergized, that is, up or down) of the track relay for that track circuit. The track circuit relay is designed to energize and pick up (indicating a vacant track) only when the coded audio frequency signal transmitted into the rails by the transmitter impedance bond for that track circuit is detected by the receiver impedance bond at the other end of the circuit. When the receiver impedance bond picks up the signal, it passes it via bond-line cables to a rack-mounted track circuit receiver module in a train control room. If the frequency and strength of the received signal fall within preset parameters, the receiver module energizes the track circuit relay for that track circuit. The energized relay signals to the ATC system that the track circuit is vacant.

When a train moves onto a track circuit, its wheelsets shunt the coded audio frequency signal away from the receiver impedance bond.[103] Absent this signal, the track circuit receiver module deenergizes the track circuit relay, allowing the relay to drop, indicating an occupied track circuit.

When train 214 entered track circuit B2-304 on the day of the accident, it should have shunted the signal away from the receiver module, and the track relay should have dropped, indicating "occupied." Once the track was detected as occupied, the ATC system should have transmitted speed commands (1) to train 214 that were appropriate to maintain a safe separation from train 110 ahead and (2) to train 112 that were appropriate to maintain separation from train 214. Instead, because the track circuit failed to detect the presence of train 214, the ATC system stopped transmitting speed commands to train 214. As a result, without either speed

---

[103] Actually, this shunting occurs slightly before a train enters the track circuit.

commands or enough momentum to carry it into the next track circuit, the train came to a stop, thus setting the stage for the accident.

After the collision, trains 214 and 112 came to rest occupying track circuit B2-304. But when investigators examined the ATC components in the train control room at the Fort Totten station,[104] they found that the relay for the track circuit was energized, indicating that the track circuit was reporting as vacant. A review of AIM historical data revealed that track circuit B2-304 had failed to detect the presence of almost every train that had passed over it on the day of the accident and for the previous 5 days, since June 17. These detection failures would have generated alarms that were self-cancelling and required no action on the part of OCC controllers.

Investigators tested track circuit B2-304 and the five circuits preceding it by placing shunts at three places along each block of track to simulate the presence of a train. For the five track circuits preceding B2-304, the ATC system correctly detected each shunt placement. But when B2-304 was tested, the ATC system reliably detected the shunt only when it was placed at the transmitter end of the track circuit.[105] The system failed to detect the shunt at all when it was placed in the middle of the circuit and only intermittently detected the shunt when it was placed at the receiver end.

The investigation determined that a failure mode was present when a series of conditions existed between the transmitter and receiver track circuit modules that generated a spurious signal of sufficient strength to be interpreted as a valid track circuit signal. First, the power output transistors of the track circuit module transmitter were producing parasitic oscillation. This oscillation was able to exploit an unintended path from the transmitter module to the respective receiver module by migrating through the equipment racks on which they were mounted. The oscillation was then coupled to the receiver module for that track circuit, producing a decaying pulse that was synchronized with the track circuit audio frequency. When the decaying pulses were of sufficient amplitude to drive the receiver module, the track circuit relay was energized, incorrectly indicating to the ATC system that the occupied track circuit was vacant.

As ATC technicians adjusted the track circuit after the June 16 and 17 installation of the US&S impedance bond for track circuit B2-304, they found that they had to increase the transmitter power level from its initial setting of 30 percent to 55 percent before the track circuit relay would reliably pick up to indicate a vacant track circuit. This increase in power level was likely necessary because of the difference in impedance of the US&S impedance bond relative to the GRS bond it replaced. The higher power level setting was well within the design operating specification of the equipment.

---

[104] The Fort Totten control room contained the ATC equipment for, among others, track circuits B2-304 and the three track circuits preceding it on track B2.

[105] In the normal direction of travel for the track, a train will pass over the receiver impedance bond as it enters a track circuit and over the transmitter bond as it leaves.

At the increased power level, the amplitude of the spurious signal became sufficient to cause the receiver module to energize the track circuit relay (to show a vacant track circuit) even while the primary audio frequency signal was being shunted by a train. Recorded data indicated that this phenomenon apparently occurred with the passage of almost every train over track circuit B2-304 from the time the impedance bond was replaced until the day of the accident. The NTSB therefore concludes that, on the day of the accident, parasitic oscillation in the track circuit modules for track circuit B2-304 was creating a spurious signal that mimicked a valid track circuit signal, thus causing the track circuit to fail to detect the presence of train 214. The NTSB further concludes that spurious signals had been causing the track circuit modules for track circuit B2-304 to erroneously indicate that the track circuit was vacant from the time the track circuit transmitter power was increased after the impedance bond was replaced on June 17, 2009, until the accident 5 days later.

The investigation found that parasitic oscillation was not unique to track circuit B2-304. The power amplifier circuits used in Metrorail's GRS track circuit modules are of the emitter-follower type, which are known to be prone to oscillate. Parasitic oscillation is a known potential problem with any amplifier circuit, which could result in the generation of unwanted additional signals, along with the intended amplified output signal. According to the manufacturer, prior to the accident it was aware of previous cases with continuous parasitic oscillation, but they had never been known to affect train detection and were considered harmless. The parasitic oscillation encountered at Fort Totten, however, was a pulse-type oscillation of sufficient amplitude and of the correct frequency to mimic the coded track occupancy signal being returned from the rails. The investigation found no evidence that the modules were tested for this type of parasitic oscillation at the time they were manufactured or installed. The WMATA train control system has exhibited failure modes that were not considered in the original design. These failure modes include parasitic oscillation, corrugated rail, and cable faults. The fail-safe design of WMATA's train control system was compromised when the track circuit modules failed to detect the presence of trains. The NTSB concludes that the track circuit modules did not function safely as part of a fail-safe train control system because GRS/Alstom did not provide a maintenance plan that would detect anomalies in the track circuit signal, such as parasitic oscillation, over the modules' service life and prevent these anomalies from being interpreted as valid track circuit signals. The NTSB recommends that Alstom Signaling Inc. conduct a comprehensive safety analysis of its audio frequency track circuit modules to evaluate all foreseeable failure modes that could cause a loss of train detection over the service life of the modules, including parasitic oscillation, and work with its customers to address these failure modes. In response to the NTSB's urgent Safety Recommendation R-09-15, which recommended examining track circuits that may be susceptible to parasitic oscillation, WMATA issued test procedure T163 and trained its ATC technicians in its use to identify parasitic oscillation. Using the T163 test procedure, engineers and technicians identified a total of 208 track circuits as having parasitic oscillation that was generated in the transmitter module. They identified 82 track circuits that exhibited parasitic oscillation in both the transmitter and the receiver modules. Eight of the 82 track circuits required corrective action to reduce the amplitude of the parasitic oscillation signal below the threshold that WMATA had established in the test procedure.

This investigation revealed that pulse-type parasitic oscillation, by mimicking a valid track circuit signal, can cause a wrong-side failure[106] of the WMATA ATC system. Although WMATA has taken action to identify track circuits with parasitic oscillation, it has not eliminated parasitic oscillation in all track circuit modules currently in service. The NTSB concludes that some of the GRS track circuit modules in use on the WMATA Metrorail system continue to exhibit parasitic oscillation, and the presence of this oscillation presents an unacceptable risk to Metrorail users. Because of the susceptibility to pulse-type parasitic oscillation that can cause a loss of train detection by the Generation 2 GRS audio frequency track circuit modules, the NTSB recommends that WMATA establish a program to permanently remove from service all of these modules within the Metrorail system. With the issuance of this recommendation, urgent Safety Recommendation R-09-15, previously classified "Open—Acceptable Response," is reclassified "Closed—Superseded."

Although WMATA's T163 procedure contains a comprehensive explanation of a parasitic oscillation failure mode and a testing protocol, the test procedure is not required to be carried out on a periodic basis. Instead, the procedure is to be carried out "as directed." The text of the procedure itself states that the procedure "or a portion or a variation" of it will be incorporated into "the future periodic maintenance program." The NTSB believes that WMATA should accelerate the process of instituting the T163 procedure as a regularly scheduled, periodic test so that parasitic oscillation can be identified and corrected before an accident occurs. Therefore, the NTSB recommends that WMATA establish periodic inspection and maintenance procedures to examine all audio frequency track circuit modules within the Metrorail system to identify and remove from service any modules that exhibit pulse-type parasitic oscillation.

Maintenance Communication System

Postaccident inspection of the maintenance communication system between the Takoma and Fort Totten stations revealed evidence that certain components of the system had been poorly maintained. For example, several inoperative telephone jacks were found in track junction boxes. The missing or unsecured telephone jacks left exposed mounting holes that could allow debris, rodents, or moisture into the box. In several instances, disconnected telephone jacks were found with bare wire terminals lying loose inside track junction boxes, and some of these were in proximity to track circuit impedance bond terminal connections. Because of this proximity and the poor condition of the terminals and boxes, the maintenance communication lines could potentially provide an alternative path for coded signals to travel from a transmitter impedance bond to a receiver bond without going through the rails (and thus bypassing any rail shunt). This alternative path could be completed through direct contact between loose wires and through the corrosion that can ground the terminals. Further, the poor condition of the nonvital communication system indicates that it is no longer of value to WMATA.

---

[106] *Wrong-side failure* refers to a failure in a railway signaling device that results in unsafe operating conditions. In this context, it may be considered the opposite of fail-safe.

Near the site of the accident, maintenance communication lines were found to be shorted to ground through corrosion inside the junction boxes, and a spectrum analyzer detected the coded signal for track circuit B2-304 on the lines. Although these signals were of insufficient strength to be recognized by the track circuit receiver module as valid signals and thus played no role in this accident, the communication lines could provide a path for signals to bypass the rails. The NTSB therefore concludes that the Metrorail maintenance communication line system—a system that was in disrepair and was apparently no longer needed by WMATA—could allow unanticipated signal paths that could degrade the integrity, and thus the safety, of the Metrorail ATC system. The NTSB recommends that WMATA completely remove the unnecessary Metrorail wayside maintenance communication system to eliminate its potential for interfering with the proper functioning of the train control system.

Routine Maintenance of Track Circuit Modules

On September 22, 2009, the NTSB issued the following safety recommendation to Alstom:

> Assist the Washington Metropolitan Area Transit Authority, and other rail transit operators and railroads that use your audio frequency track circuit equipment, in examining their train control systems for susceptibility to parasitic oscillations and spurious signals capable of exploiting unintended signal paths, and implementing measures to eliminate those adverse conditions that could affect the safe performance of their train control systems. (R-09-23 Urgent)

The manufacturer-recommended maintenance schedule for the GRS track circuit modules used by WMATA outlines a series of tests involving the measurement of average and peak-to-peak voltage levels and certain operating frequencies. These measurements are designed to ensure that the track circuit transmitter and receiver modules are operating at reasonable power and sensitivity levels and within published frequency tolerances. This maintenance schedule does not specify the measurement of detailed signal waveform parameters, such as total harmonic distortion and spectral frequency distribution, that would have revealed the presence of parasitic oscillation.

Only one procedure calls for the use of an oscilloscope capable of detailed signal waveform measurement. This procedure only calls for simple peak-to-peak voltage measurement and sets no minimum vertical bandwidth requirement on the oscilloscope to be used. Most important, recommended maintenance contains no discussion of tests designed to determine the presence of spurious signals that could mimic a valid track circuit signal. The NTSB concludes that a technician following the manufacturer-provided GRS track circuit module maintenance procedures would not have detected the spurious signals that caused track circuit B2-304 to fail in an unsafe manner.

On June 26, 2010, Alstom informed the NTSB that it was continuing to evaluate strategies for mitigating the pulse-type parasitic oscillation found in the Generation 2 GRS modules at Fort Totten. Alstom also told the NTSB that it had contacted other transit agencies known to be using Generation 2 GRS modules and that it had done limited testing at each site to identify modules exhibiting behavior similar to the modules at Fort Totten. Alstom has also developed a new procedure and test equipment that the company says it will use to test all the known Generation 2 GRS modules currently in service across the country. Although the NTSB welcomes this effort, it believes that in addition to one-time testing, rail transit operators that use GRS audio frequency track circuit equipment should be provided with maintenance guidelines that ensure that the ATC system is properly maintained over time. The NTSB therefore recommends that Alstom develop and implement periodic inspection and maintenance guidelines for use by WMATA and other rail transit operators and railroads equipped with GRS audio frequency track circuit modules and assist them in identifying and removing from service all modules that exhibit pulse-type parasitic oscillation in order to ensure the vitality and integrity of the ATC system.

In May of 2010, the NTSB contacted several transit agencies that use GRS audio frequency track circuit modules similar to those used by WMATA. Some of those agencies told the NTSB that they have asked Alstom to provide them with guidelines to test for parasitic oscillation so that such tests can be incorporated into their track circuit inspection and maintenance programs. They also reported that Alstom had not responded to their requests; however, Alstom notified the NTSB on June 26, 2010, that "Alstom is in the process of arranging site visits to all of its customers using Generation 2 modules to test and document the condition of all the identified track circuits." Therefore, the NTSB recommends that the six other rail transit agencies[107] that use GRS audio frequency track circuit modules work with Alstom to establish periodic inspection and maintenance procedures to examine all GRS audio frequency track circuit modules to identify and remove from service any modules that exhibit pulse-type parasitic oscillation. With the issuance of this recommendation and the related recommendation to Alstom, urgent Safety Recommendation R-09-23, previously classified "Open—Acceptable Response," is reclassified "Closed—Superseded."

The NTSB is not aware of any other transit properties experiencing pulse-type parasitic oscillation. Alstom has informed the NTSB that it has not found pulse-type parasitic oscillation on other transit properties that use its equipment. Ansaldo has informed the NTSB that it has implemented strategies to prevent parasitic oscillation in the design of the Ansaldo/US&S track circuit modules and that no evidence of parasitic oscillation has been found in these modules.

WMATA is currently supplementing the manufacturer-recommended maintenance schedule with testing developed by WMATA ATC engineers (outlined in T163–*GRS ATP Module Parasitic Oscillation Test*) after parasitic oscillation was discovered in the Fort Totten track circuit modules. These tests include detailed measurement of transmit signal waveform parameters used to identify the presence of harmful parasitic oscillation and to diagnose its severity. The T163 test specifies that corrective action is required only in the case where code-rate modulated parasitic oscillation is present in the module of the associated track circuit

---

[107] Massachusetts Bay Transportation Authority, Southeastern Pennsylvania Transportation Authority, Greater Cleveland Regional Transit Authority, Metropolitan Atlanta Regional Transportation Authority, Los Angeles County Metropolitan Transportation Authority, and Chicago Transit Authority.

receiver and this oscillation exists above a certain amplitude threshold. This defines the case in which a spurious signal capable of mimicking a valid track circuit signal has propagated to the associated track circuit receiver and is present in that module with sufficient amplitude to cause concern for future loss of train detection. The WMATA maintenance schedule specifies that the T163 test be performed on an as-directed basis.

WMATA ATC engineers are currently using a modified version of the original loss-of-shunt tool to monitor anomalies in track circuit operation. This monitoring is performed twice per day and encompasses all of the track circuit occupancy data collected over the previous 24 hours. Any anomalous behavior indicative of a loss of train detection is flagged and results in direction to use the T163 test to diagnose the condition of the track circuit. The NTSB concludes that WMATA Metrorail ATC test procedure T163, developed since this accident, will permit technicians to detect the presence of parasitic oscillation like that found in the failed track circuit modules at Fort Totten; however, unless these procedures are carried out on a periodic basis, an unsafe condition may persist for some time before being discovered and corrected.

In Safety Recommendation R-09-16, issued during this accident investigation, the NTSB made the following recommendation to WMATA:

> Develop a program to periodically determine that electronic components in your train control system are performing within design tolerances. (R-09-16)

In its June 11, 2010, response to Safety Recommendation R-09-16, WMATA offered that its T163 procedure met the intent of this recommendation. However, the T163 procedure only tests for parasitic oscillation and it does not specify periodic testing to detect changes in the operating characteristics of electronic components within the track circuit modules. Pending further information from WMATA with regard to its plans for developing a periodic preventive inspection and maintenance program to monitor the operating tolerances of the electronic components in the train control system, Safety Recommendation R-09-16 remains classified "Open—Acceptable Response."

The manufacturer-provided maintenance schedule outlines a quarterly series of activities that would help determine if the operation of the track circuit module has drifted too far from the original design operating point. To better monitor track circuit performance between scheduled tests, WMATA ATC engineers developed the loss-of-shunt tool. This tool effectively extends the quarterly shunt test to additional points in time using data collected during normal revenue operation and with actual trains performing the shunting. If the underlying analog characteristics and operating point of a track circuit were to deviate from the original design specifications, the frequency of incorrect track circuit "occupied"/"unoccupied" decisions will change. The loss-of-shunt tool provides WMATA with a way to monitor this statistic and help to identify track circuits in need of adjustment or repair. However, because the loss-of-shunt tool is designed to operate only on historical data, it cannot identify detrimental changes in track circuit operation until after a failure to properly identify the presence of a train has already occurred. After the accident, WMATA began reviewing the loss-of-shunt information twice per day. It is also working to develop a real-time train detection system using track occupancy data.

ATC System Design

The WMATA signal and train control system was designed using the closed-loop[108] and fail-safe principles that have been used in the rail industry for decades. Under closed-loop and fail-safe design principles, a single-point failure of a logical operation or the absence of a required input or output should not result in an unsafe condition.

The WMATA ATO and ATP subsystems are referred to as "vital" or "safety-critical." Satisfying the design criteria for a vital train control system requires that if a track circuit fails to indicate correspondence with conditions at the wayside, the circuit should default to the safest condition, which is to indicate the presence of a train even when the block is actually unoccupied. This investigation determined that the fail-safe design principle can be compromised in the WMATA train control system as a result of two different conditions—the presence of corrugated rail and the presence of pulse-type parasitic oscillation in the track circuit transmitters.

Electrical arcing in the presence of corrugated rail can create harmonics that effectively mimic a valid track circuit signal that can be accepted by the receiver via the normal signal path. Parasitic oscillation in track circuit transmitters can create a spurious signal that effectively mimics the track circuit signal by entering the receiver via an unintended signal path. In each case, the receiver module detects a signal that it interprets as valid. WMATA ATC engineers consider harmonics resulting from corrugated rail to be a benign condition because of their transient nature. However, the NTSB believes that any condition that can result in a loss of train detection needs to be evaluated in a comprehensive safety analysis.

Examination of wayside junction boxes also revealed that WMATA maintenance communication system cables were co-located with track circuit cables. This design could potentially lead to the creation of an unintended signal path that could affect the operation of the track circuit system. For example, the maintenance communication system cables had become grounded due to corrosion, providing a potential alternative track circuit signal path. Also, loose cables in the junction boxes could possibly come into contact with a cable used by the track circuit and thereby establish an unintended track circuit signal path.

A key requirement of the fail-safe design approach is that the designer foresee all catastrophic failure modes in the system and develop a plan for mitigating the negative effects that such failure modes can have on system function. A comprehensive safety analysis of the system design, which considers all known failure modes, their effects on system function, and the timely detection and alerting of failures is critical to developing an effective mitigation plan. A June 1980 fault tree analysis performed for WMATA identified events that could lead to train collisions, but it did not explore failure modes involving the track circuitry, nor did it identify the possibility of parasitic oscillation in the track circuit modules. As a result, there was no plan to mitigate the effects of such failures on the WMATA ATC system.

---

[108] The *closed-loop* principle requires that all conditions necessary for the existence of any permissive state or action be verified to be present before the permissive state or action can be initiated or maintained.

The NTSB concludes that a comprehensive safety analysis of an ATC system must consider all foreseeable system failures that may result in a loss of train separation, including failures in train detection caused by track circuit failures. The NTSB recommends that WMATA conduct a comprehensive safety analysis of the Metrorail ATC system to evaluate all foreseeable failures of this system that could result in a loss of train separation, and work with your train control equipment manufacturers to address in that analysis all potential failure modes that could cause a loss of train detection, including parasitic oscillation, cable faults and placement, and corrugated rail. The NTSB further recommends that based on the findings of the safety analysis recommended in the previous recommendation, WMATA should incorporate the design, operational, and maintenance controls necessary to address potential failures in the ATC system.

Another safety design strategy is redundancy, which typically refers to the provision of an independent backup for the function of a particular part or system in cases of unforeseen failure modes. For a train control system, redundancy can be provided by such means as an independent backup track circuit system, a system that tracks train locations to help prevent collisions, or a real-time monitoring system for detection and warning of track circuit failures. This investigation revealed that WMATA's train control system was generating historical track occupancy data, but the data were not being effectively used to monitor track circuit performance. Accordingly, the NTSB recommended in its July 13, 2009, urgent Safety Recommendation R-09-6 that WMATA enhance the safety redundancy of its train control system by evaluating track occupancy data on a real-time basis in order to detect losses in track occupancy and automatically generate alerts to prevent collisions.

Tests and Maintenance Preceding Accident

At the time of the accident, WMATA had recently completed long-term programs to increase Metrorail traction power (so the system could accommodate longer, heavier trains) and was still replacing critical ATC system components, many of which date back to the origins of the Metrorail system in the mid-1970s. This program involved replacing older GRS components with components supplied by US&S.

On December 12, 2007, as part of the traction power upgrade program, WMATA ATC technicians replaced the GRS impedance bond at chain marker 311+71 on track B2 with a US&S impedance bond. This bond served as the receiver impedance bond for track circuit B2-304 and the transmitter impedance bond for adjacent track circuit B2-312. Train control room logs for that date indicated that the installation crew performed a verification test to make sure the track circuits were working properly before they left the area. But a review of AIM system historical data showed that about 6:30 a.m. on December 12, 2007, shortly after completion of the installation of the new impedance bond, track circuit B2-304 began bobbing (showing false train occupancies) between train movements.

About 2 1/2 months later, on February 28, 2008, a work order was opened for track circuit B2-304 because of bobbing. The work order was closed on September 26, 2008; the work order entries did not indicate what actions had been taken to correct the problem. A review of

AIM system historical records showed that intermittent bobbing continued to occur on the track circuit.

Five days before the accident, on June 17, 2009, WMATA ATC mechanics replaced the GRS transmitter impedance bond for track circuit B2-304 with a US&S bond. According to the installation crew leader, as the final track circuit adjustments were being made, the B2-304 track circuit began bobbing, along with the adjacent track circuit B2-312. She said she reported the bobbing track circuits to the MOC, then the crew left the area. At 6:50 a.m., the MOC opened a work order for bobbing track circuit B2-304 (but not for bobbing track circuit B2-312).

The next day, June 18, 2009, a Red Line maintenance crew performed routine, scheduled preventive maintenance in the area of the replaced impedance bond. After completing shunt testing of track circuit B2-304, the crew noted that the track circuit was bobbing. Members of the maintenance crew said they had not been aware of the open work order regarding the track circuit, and they did not report the bobbing because the problem had apparently cleared itself while they were troubleshooting.

According to AIM system data, train detection failed for almost every train that occupied track circuit B2-304 from the time the impedance bond was replaced on June 17, 2009, until the accident on June 22.

No record was found that train operators traversing the area reported any problem with track circuit B2-304 during this period, even though almost all of them experienced a loss of speed commands, even if temporarily, as they passed over it. However, unless, like train 214, a train comes to a stop fully within the boundaries of the track circuit, the speed commands will return as the train's momentum carries it onto the next track circuit where its presence is properly detected. In the case of train 214, the operator attributed his loss of speed commands to his proximity to train 110 that he was following; he did not interpret it as the train control system malfunction that it actually represented.

The NTSB concludes that train operators did not report problems with track circuit B2-304 before the accident because reductions in speed commands to maintain train separation, or even momentary losses of all speed commands, were common during train operations.

Using Track Circuit Components from Different Manufacturers

As discussed previously, the process used by WMATA to carry out its track circuit replacement program involved the use of US&S impedance bonds with GRS track circuit modules. Such a combination of components from different manufacturers was in place for track circuit B2-304 at the time of the accident.

In a 2004 letter to its customers, Alstom (the vendor for the GRS components) advised against the use of third-party components with Alstom products unless a thorough engineering analysis had been performed beforehand. Additionally, postaccident interviews revealed that Alstom's manager of train detection products had told WMATA that Alstom could not endorse the use of US&S bonds with GRS modules. The WMATA ATC engineer said that the Alstom manager had told him that he could not endorse using equipment from different manufacturers because he did not know the characteristics of the other components.

The WMATA ATC systems engineer who had been involved in the track circuit replacement program from the beginning identified through bench tests an approximate 10-percent difference in resistive impedance between the US&S and GRS impedance bonds. When he connected a GRS module to a US&S impedance bond he found no significant deviation from what would be expected from a circuit using all GRS components. Further, track circuits using components from both manufacturers were successfully tested at three locations in rail yards to confirm that no incompatibilities existed that would affect reliability.

The NTSB considered whether the failure that led to the collision at Fort Totten could have resulted from the use of incompatible track circuit components. No evidence was found that track circuit B2-304 had been failing to detect trains immediately before the impedance bond was replaced on June 17, 2009, whereas after the replacement and subsequent track circuit adjustment, track occupancy detection began to fail and continued to do so up through the day of the accident. Additionally, track circuit B1-245 began to malfunction after the receiver impedance bond was replaced.

The investigation reviewed the impedance bond replacement activity for track circuit B1-245 and found that the losses of train detection that occurred after the receiver bond was replaced with a US&S bond coincided with a change in the transmitter power level setting. The behavior of track circuit B1-245 was similar to the behavior of the Fort Totten track circuit in which parasitic oscillation was present that caused a loss of train detection. A review of data from the loss-of-shunt tool indicated that after both GRS track circuit modules were replaced, there were no further losses of train detection in this track circuit.

The problem identified with the malfunctioning track circuit B2-304 was the presence of parasitic oscillation generated by the transmitter module that migrated through the rack structure to the receiver module. Between September and October 2009, after identifying the track circuit failure mode in the Fort Totten accident, WMATA ATC engineers tested 96 track circuits that had exhibited possible loss-of-shunt events. Twenty track circuits were identified as exhibiting the pulse-type oscillation similar to the oscillation seen in the Fort Totten modules. All 20 of these track circuits were equipped with GRS impedance bonds and GRS track circuit modules.

The investigation determined that the US&S impedance bond and the bond it replaced were functionally equivalent. About one-third of the time, according to WMATA ATC personnel, the replacement of GRS bonds with US&S bonds required that the transmitter power be increased in order to provide sufficient signal strength to be acted upon by the receiver module. The increases in power level that were required were within the design parameters of the modules and, absent parasitic oscillation, should not have interfered with the ability of the track circuit to accurately detect trains.

No evidence was offered that before this accident Alstom had done any engineering analysis that revealed an incompatibility between US&S impedance bonds and GRS track circuit modules. The September 2004 Alstom letter to its customers regarding the use of non-OEM equipment did not specifically address the components at issue in this investigation. Although it is understandable that Alstom would be unwilling to accept responsibility for the performance of any components the company had neither provided nor proven through its own engineering evaluation, the company's 2004 letter does not contain any information relevant to the compatibility or incompatibility of the US&S bonds and GRS modules.

Several of the ATC technicians interviewed during this investigation voiced concerns about the compatibility of the US&S and GRS components and suggested that such concerns were shared by other technicians. They referred to frequent problems that they had encountered after a new bond installation, and they attributed these problems to incompatibility of components from different manufacturers. However, the investigation found that the problems mentioned by the ATC technicians generally involved the perceived failure of the installation crews to properly adjust the speed command signals when they made the postinstallation track circuit adjustments. None of the technicians were involved in the assessment by WMATA engineers of the compatibility of the US&S and GRS components.

The investigation determined that latent pulse-type parasitic oscillation existed in a number of other track circuits, all of which consisted entirely of GRS components. Between the end of October and the end of December 2009, WMATA tested all Metrorail track circuits to identify those with parasitic oscillation that could cause the circuit to fail to detect the presence of trains. A total of 82 track circuits were so identified, and corrective measures were taken. All of these circuits used GRS impedance bonds and GRS track circuit modules, so incompatibility of components was not a factor in these cases.

After the Fort Totten accident, investigators conducted laboratory tests on the track circuit modules that had been in place at the Rosslyn station when a failure of train detection in track circuit C2-111 almost led to two rear-end collisions in 2005. At certain power levels, these modules also exhibited parasitic oscillation similar to the oscillation found in the Fort Totten modules after this accident. The presence of these oscillations was consistent with the noise on the peaks of the track circuit signal wave form that the ATC systems engineer said he observed during his 2005 examination of the Rosslyn modules. A review of the data records for track circuit C2-111 showed that, for the entire time period for which the records existed (beginning in 1988), the track circuit had periodically failed to detect the presence of a train occupying the circuit. This track circuit had always used GRS impedance bonds with GRS modules.

Finally, WMATA reported that in 26 track circuits, GRS impedance bonds had been replaced with high-current US&S bonds as part of the traction power upgrade program. None of these track circuits with components from different manufacturers showed evidence of train detection anomalies. The NTSB concludes that as shown by the fact that (1) the GRS modules in the accident track circuit B2-304 consistently exhibited parasitic oscillation in on-scene and laboratory testing regardless of the type of impedance bond or simulated load used, (2) numerous other Metrorail track circuits that used all GRS components were found to have parasitic oscillation similar to the oscillation found at Fort Totten, and (3) numerous other track circuits with components made by different manufacturers showed no evidence of such oscillation, this accident did not result from WMATA's use of US&S impedance bonds with GRS track circuit modules. The NTSB further concludes that the change in transmitter power level necessitated by the installation of a US&S impedance bond in track circuit B2-304 was within the design parameters of the equipment and would not have resulted in a failure of train detection in the absence of parasitic oscillation within the GRS track circuit modules.

Implementation of ATC Test and Inspection Procedures

Four years before the Fort Totten accident, the WMATA Metrorail investigation of the two near-collisions occurring between the Rosslyn and Foggy Bottom stations determined that a track circuit had failed to detect trains occupying it. The investigation also revealed that a malfunctioning track circuit could pass a shunt verification test and detect the shunt when it was placed at either end of the circuit, but fail to detect the shunt when it was placed in the middle of the circuit.

Based on this finding, WMATA, on June 19, 2005, issued engineering bulletin and ATC safety notice *Update on Diminished Shunt Sensitivity in Audio Frequency Track Circuits* that stated that verification of audio frequency track circuits must involve placement of a shunt in the middle of the track circuit as well as near the transmitter end. This represented a change from the existing procedures (PMI 11000), which allowed use of a single shunt placed inside the transmitter end of the track circuit for verification. None of the ATC personnel (five technicians and one supervisor) interviewed during this accident investigation were familiar with the June 19, 2005, bulletin or the requirement to verify a track circuit by placing a shunt in the middle of the circuit, even though all of them were working as Metrorail ATC technicians when the Rosslyn incident occurred. This included technicians who were responsible for verifying track circuits after work had been performed, as well as those who were responsible for performing scheduled preventive maintenance inspections.

According to WMATA, the October 6, 2006, engineering bulletin and safety notice regarding track circuit verification, *US&S Impedance Bonds in GRS ATP Track Circuits,* was intended to address concerns raised by some ATC technicians regarding the use of US&S impedance bonds with GRS modules. That safety notice stated that if a track circuit does not pass a three-shunt verification process (involving shunt placements at each end and in the middle of track circuits), the original impedance bond should be reinstalled. None of the technicians interviewed appeared familiar with the October 6, 2006, bulletin regarding three-point shunt verification after installation of US&S impedance bonds. The supervisor of the installation crew was familiar with the bulletin, but he mistakenly believed that it referred only to high-current impedance bonds.

At the public hearing on this accident, the WMATA communications superintendent acknowledged that, during the 2005–2006 time frame, the process by which engineering and technical bulletins was distributed was "uneven." Given that no technician interviewed during this investigation was familiar with the June 2005 procedures for verifying track circuits and only one was even vaguely aware of the October 6, 2006, bulletin, the bulletin distribution process was clearly ineffective.

For 5 years before this accident, WMATA engineers had known that attempting to verify a track circuit without placing a shunt in the middle of the circuit could result in a failure to identify malfunctioning circuits. But WMATA did not ensure that this information was provided to and understood by all ATC technicians and that the technicians subsequently acted upon it.

Although the leader of the crew that installed the US&S bond for track circuit B2-304 shortly before the accident said that her crew had verified the track circuit using three shunts, one of which would presumably have been in the middle of the circuit, she could not provide a reason for using three shunts other than personal preference. In addition, NTSB testing found that track circuit B2-304 consistently failed to detect a shunt placed in the middle of the circuit, suggesting that if the impedance bond installation crew did use three shunt placements to verify the track circuit, these shunt placements did not include placing a shunt in the middle of the circuit. The NTSB therefore concludes that if proper shunt placements had been used, as required by WMATA's procedures, to verify track circuit B2-304 either immediately after the new impedance bond was installed on June 17, 2009, or when the track circuit was tested the following day, the work crews would have been able to determine that the track circuit was failing to detect trains, and actions could have been taken to resolve the problem and prevent the accident.

Based on NTSB testing, even a two-shunt verification test that involved placement of a shunt at the middle of the track circuit (in accordance with the guidance developed after the 2005 Rosslyn incident) would have shown that track circuit B2-304 would fail to detect trains. The NTSB concludes that WMATA failed to institutionalize and employ systemwide the enhanced track circuit verification test developed following the 2005 Rosslyn near-collisions, and this test procedure, had it been formally implemented, would have been sufficient to identify track circuits that could fail in the manner of those at Rosslyn and Fort Totten. During its investigation of a 1996 collision between a Metrorail train and an empty standing train at the Shady Grove station,[109] the NTSB identified deficiencies in Metrorail's procedures for disseminating information to operating personnel. Based on those findings, the NTSB made the following safety recommendation to WMATA:

> Develop and implement procedures to ensure that Metrorail operations personnel receive all bulletins, special orders, memoranda, or notices related to their responsibilities. These procedures should include a mechanism by which these personnel must sign or initial a document to signify that they have received, read, and understood any guidance intended for them. (R-96-34)

WMATA responded that it had adopted General Rule 1.7a, which requires acknowledgment, by signature, that an employee has received, reviewed, and understood new or

---

[109] NTSB/RAR-96/04.

modified rules, operating procedures, and safety-related postings or bulletins. Based on this response, the NTSB classified Safety Recommendation R-96-34 "Closed—Acceptable Action" on August 18, 1997.

As revealed during this investigation, however, WMATA has not effectively addressed the issues raised in the 1996 investigation of the Shady Grove accident. Although, according to public hearing testimony, WMATA does require employees to sign for updated bulletins and notices, the agency does not have mechanisms in place to ensure that the employees understand or act on the information. Assuming the ATC technicians interviewed in this investigation did receive and sign for the 2005 and 2006 bulletins having to do with shunt placement (these records are retained for only 2 years and could not be produced for this investigation), their procedures did not change as a result. The technicians would have had no reason to ignore the new or updated procedures, which makes it likely that they failed to receive or understand the significance of the information. If that was the case, some followup action on the part of WMATA management to determine if the revised procedures were being followed would have revealed it. But no such action was taken. The NTSB therefore concludes that WMATA did not effectively distribute technical bulletins and safety information to its ATC technicians nor did it ensure that the information was received, understood, and properly acted upon by those technicians. The NTSB therefore recommends that WMATA review the process by which Metrorail technical bulletins and other safety information are provided to employees and revise that process as necessary to ensure that (1) employees have received the information intended for them, (2) employees understand the actions to be taken in response to the information, and (3) employees take the appropriate actions.

Insulation Resistance Testing

The Metrorail ATC technical procedure T031, *Cable Insulation Resistance Testing*, dated November 25, 2008, was in draft form and under review at the time of this accident. This was a new manual with requirements for cable insulation resistance testing that previously had not been in place. WMATA representatives told the NTSB that no insulation resistance testing of cables had been conducted on the Metrorail system.

This draft technical procedure would require that all cables installed in conduits, in ducts, and along tunnel walls, or buried along the right-of-way, and wires and cables entering and leaving train control rooms, equipment cases, and junction boxes be measured for insulation resistance. The tests are intended to verify that the insulation resistance of a conductor used with a power source of less than 600 volts exceeds 1 megaohm and that the resistance of a conductor used with a power source greater than 600 volts exceeds 10 megaohms. This draft procedure requires that the applicable wires and cables be tested every 10 years or after new installations.

When investigators tested the insulation resistance of the cables serving the two impedance bonds of track circuit B2-304, they found resistance measurements that did not meet the standards spelled out in procedure T031. For the tested cables, insulation resistance was 500 kiloohms, or only half of the resistance required by procedure T031 for a power source of less than 600 volts. The NTSB therefore concludes that, as revealed by postaccident testing, the cables serving the impedance bonds for track circuit B2-304 did not meet proposed WMATA Metrorail standards for insulation resistance, and although this did not cause or contribute to the accident, such deficiencies, if undetected and uncorrected, could undermine the safety of the Metrorail train control system. The NTSB therefore recommends that WMATA implement cable insulation resistance testing as part of Metrorail's periodic maintenance program.

Safety Culture

The NTSB has on a number of occasions recognized the lack of an organizational culture of safety within a transportation agency as having contributed to an accident.[110] Organizations with effective safety cultures are generally described as having a commitment to safety that permeates the entire organization; that is, senior management demonstrates a commitment to safety and a concern for hazards that are shared by employees at all levels within the organization. In order for an organization like WMATA, which relies heavily on technology, to maintain an effective safety culture, senior managers must continuously review their organization's performance and practices through monitoring, analysis, and feedback systems.[111] When safety deficiencies are identified, the problems and the mitigation procedures must be communicated to all affected personnel in the organization.

Research on organizations that have demonstrated successful safety records operating in complex, high-risk environments—sometimes referred to as high-reliability organizations (HRO)—has identified some common characteristics in these organizations' approach to risk. Commonalities include an avoidance of trial-and-error learning and constant concern with unforeseen problems.[112]

Testimony was given during the public hearing on this accident by three panelists who had either conducted research on or applied HRO concepts in government or industry. One panelist characterized an HRO as "a learning organization":

> ... an organization that repeatedly accomplishes its high-hazard mission while avoiding catastrophic events, despite ... consequential hazards, very dynamic tasks, time constraints, and complex technologies ... a key component of being an HRO is ... learning from [the organization's] ... mistakes ....

Another panelist said

---

[110] For example, see (a) *Wheels-Up Landing Continental Airlines Flight 1943 Douglas DC-9 N10556 Houston, Texas, February 19, 1996*, Aircraft Accident Report NTSB/AAR-97/01 (Washington, DC: National Transportation Safety Board, 1997); (b) *Controlled Flight into Terrain Federal Aviation Administration Beech Super King Air 300/F,N82, Front Royal, Virginia, October 28, 1993*, Aircraft Accident Report NTSB/AAR-94/03 (Washington, DC: National Transportation Safety Board, 1994); (c) NTSB/RAR-96/04.

[111] N. Pidgeon and M. O'Leary, "Man-Made Disasters: Why Technology and Organizations (sometimes) Fail," *Safety Science*, vol. 34 (2000), pp. 15–30.

[112] K. E. Weick and K. M. Sutcliffe, *Managing the Unexpected—Assuring High Performance in an Age of Complexity* (San Francisco: Jossey-Bass, 2001).

The new way of thinking is that human error is a symptom of trouble deeper in the system, and that is an attitudinal shift that is necessary for people to really understand how high-reliability organizations can function.

Safety Culture Issues Within WMATA

An exhibit from the public hearing on this accident was a copy of a June 25, 2009, presentation to the WMATA Board of Directors from the WMATA Customer Services, Operations, and Safety Committee. The presentation included the statement, "Metro continues to influence a positive safety culture by taking immediate actions to correct recognized hazards." Examples of safety indicators in the presentation included station and parking lot injuries and escalator injuries, which are not directly related to the safety of train operations. Also mentioned were derailments, smoke and fire events, and improper door operations that are more relevant to train operations. However, the presentation did not address progress on TOC safety audit findings, open CAPs, or FTA and NTSB recommendations—despite a requirement in the WMATA system safety program plan that such information be regularly provided by the WMATA general manager to the Board of Directors. The NTSB is concerned that WMATA senior management may have placed too much emphasis on investigating events such as station and escalator injuries to the exclusion of passenger safety during transit.

The safety initiatives touted by the Customer Services, Operations, and Safety Committee, the language used, and the oversight and enforcement methods are indicative of a model of safety management focused on unsafe acts and procedural violations by individuals. Definitions included in the WMATA safety presentation characterized a preventable accident as "an accident that occurred because the employee failed to do everything reasonably expected of a trained professional to avoid involvement in an accident." A nonpreventable accident is "an accident that occurs despite every reasonable action by the employee to avoid involvement in an accident." Safety initiatives cited in the presentation included training personnel, posting signs, and making frequent reminders to personnel. Based on the information contained in this presentation, before the Fort Totten accident, WMATA placed much of the blame for causing and much of the responsibility for preventing accidents on frontline personnel. As will be discussed with regard to just culture, placing blame on frontline employees is not likely to improve the safety of the system as a whole.

Such person-centered approaches to safety are well suited to high-risk environments in which unsafe acts by individuals can result in injury to those directly involved. Risks faced by some WMATA employees—risks to trackside workers, for example—clearly fall into this category. In the Fort Totten accident, however, the accident did not result from the actions of an individual but from the "accumulation of latent conditions within the maintenance, managerial and organizational spheres" making it an example of a "quintessential organizational accident."[113] Organizational conditions can contribute to employee accidents and workplace

---

[113] J. Reason, *Managing the Risks of Organizational Accidents* (Aldershot: Ashgate, 1997) and J. Reason, "Achieving a Safe Culture: Theory and Practice," *Work and Stress*, vol. 12 (1998), p. 227.

injuries, but tracking and preventing workplace injuries and unsafe acts by individuals does not predict or prevent organizational accidents.

WMATA's focus, before the accident, on individuals rather than on the system as a whole is exemplified by one Red Line ATC technician's description of the organization's safety procedures:

> We used to have meetings with our superintendent in our department. We used to be able to gripe about our complaints. But now all we get is rule, rule, rule. When something happens, they're so reactive rather than let's sit down [and] talk about this, let's discuss this. And it's more reaction when something goes wrong than just trying to prevent something from happening.

In addition to focusing on individual behaviors rather than systemwide safety issues, FTA audits found that WMATA and its oversight authority, TOC, were unable to adequately identify and address system safety deficiencies as required by 49 CFR Part 659.

The 2005 FTA audit of TOC focused on the ability of TOC to develop and implement plans and procedures required for the implementation of 49 CFR Part 659. As a result of this audit, the FTA issued nine deficiency findings and one recommendation regarding TOC's implementation of 49 CFR Part 659 requirements. Over the next 2 years, TOC and WMATA were unable to close several of these audit findings, prompting the FTA to conduct a series of meetings with TOC and WMATA executive leadership. The FTA was concerned about WMATA's ability to identify, elevate, and address safety deficiencies within its own agency as well as WMATA's lack of responsiveness to TOC.

Therefore, the NTSB concludes that, before the accident, the WMATA Board of Directors did not seek adequate information about, nor did it demonstrate adequate oversight to address, the number of open CAPs from previous TOC and FTA safety audits of WMATA. The NTSB recommends that WMATA develop a formal process by which the general manager and managers responsible for WMATA operations, maintenance, and engineering will periodically review, in collaboration with the chief safety officer, all safety audits and open CAPs, and modify policy, identify and commit resources, and initiate any other action necessary to ensure that the plans are adequately addressed and closed within the required time frame. The NTSB also concludes that the WMATA Board of Directors did not exercise oversight responsibility for the system safety of the WMATA system. Therefore, the NTSB recommends that the WMATA Board of Directors elevate the safety oversight role of the WMATA Board of Directors by (1) developing a policy statement to explicitly and publicly assume the responsibility for continual oversight of system safety, (2) implementing processes to exercise oversight of system safety, including appropriate proactive performance metrics, and (3) evaluating actions taken in response to NTSB and FTA recommendations, as well as the status of open CAPs and the results of audits conducted by TOC.

The failure of WMATA engineers and technicians or managers to properly address track circuit anomalies is symptomatic of the larger safety culture issues within the organization. After the impedance bond was replaced on June 17 and the track circuit began bobbing, the ATC crew that had performed the installation and subsequent track circuit adjustment left the area with the problem unresolved. The crew leader reported at least one of the bobbing track circuits (B2-304) to the MOC, and she expected that the MOC would forward the information to the next crew. The MOC opened a work order for the bobbing track circuit, but it took no other immediate action. During the public hearing for this accident, the WMATA superintendent of communications stated that this work order was 1 of 10 corrective maintenance work orders open on the Red Line at the time and he acknowledged that problems that affected train movements took priority. Bobbing track circuits were not considered by WMATA to affect the safety of train movements despite the fact that Metrorail trains will operate safely in automatic mode only as long as the presence of those trains is accurately detected by each track circuit they occupy.

On June 18, 2009, the day after the new impedance bond was installed and the work order was opened, ATC technicians conducted a preventive maintenance inspection in an area that included track circuit B2-304. The technicians verified the track circuit by using a single shunt, but they found that the track circuit was bobbing. They noted the bobbing in the train control room logbook, but they did not notify the MOC because the weather was deteriorating and the track circuit had passed the verification test. The technicians thus performed a test of the track circuit and found problems with it, but they took no action to see that the problem was addressed. ATC technicians said that they assumed the bond installation crew would return to the site to continue work, but they had no basis for this assumption.

The safety behaviors and attitudes of individuals are influenced by their perceptions and expectations about safety in their work environment,[114] and they pattern their safety behaviors to meet demonstrated priorities of organizational leaders, regardless of stated policies.[115] Statements made by the supervisor of the CIT installation crew in a postaccident interview are indicative of an emphasis on maintaining operations over safety. The supervisor said, "If the track circuit's bobbing, normal procedure is [that it] … be worked on. If there's a crew changeover, it's still to be worked on." However, the NTSB notes that he also said that "the mentality now is move trains."

The apparent tendency among many managers to tolerate various failures and malfunctions in the ATC system was also likely influenced by their perceptions of past system performance. This may explain why WMATA officials had designated track circuit alarms in the OCC as requiring no specific response and why neither WMATA ATC technicians nor maintenance officials placed a high priority on addressing track circuit bobbing and loss of train detection. The NTSB concludes that the low priority that WMATA Metrorail managers placed on addressing malfunctions in the train control system before the accident likely influenced the

[114] D. Zohar, "Safety Climate in Industrial Organizations: Theoretical and Applied Implications," *Journal of Applied Psychology*, vol. 65 (1980), pp. 96–102.

[115] D. Zohar, "A Group-level Model of Safety Climate: Testing the Effect of Group Climate on Micro-accidents in Manufacturing Jobs," *Journal of Applied Psychology*, vol. 85 (2000), pp. 587–596 and D. Zohar, "The Effects of Leadership Dimensions, Safety Climate, and Assigned Priorities on Minor Injuries in Work Groups," *Journal of Organizational Behavior*, vol. 23 (2000), pp. 75–92.

inadequate response to such malfunctions by ATC technicians, OCC controllers, and train operators.

The NTSB notes that since the Fort Totten accident, WMATA has taken steps to ensure that its track circuits accurately detect the presence of trains. WMATA has increased the use of the loss-of-shunt tool to monitor track circuit performance and is working to improve the effectiveness of the tool. WMATA has developed procedures under which engineering staff are immediately notified when a potential malfunction occurs. The NTSB concludes that the steps that WMATA has taken since the Fort Totten accident, such as improving and increasing the use of the loss-of-shunt software tool for identifying track circuit malfunctions, will contribute to improving the safety of the system. However, these steps are just the beginning of the process that WMATA should undertake to develop a more effective safety culture.

Characteristics of an Effective Safety Culture

A commonly cited model of an effective safety culture is that offered by Dr. James Reason, who describes a safety culture as (1) an *informed culture* in which those who operate and manage the system have knowledge about the human, technical, organizational, and environmental factors affecting the safety of the system; (2) a *reporting culture* in which people are able and encouraged to report safety concerns, errors, and near-misses; and (3) a *just culture* in which people are encouraged and rewarded for providing safety-related information without fear of blame.[116] Reason further characterizes an effective safety culture as a *flexible culture* that can break from a conventional management hierarchy when needed to handle safety concerns and a *learning culture* that has the willingness and competence to draw the right conclusions from its safety information and to implement whatever reforms are necessary to address identified safety issues.

Informed Culture. An informed culture is characterized as

one in which those who manage and operate the system have current knowledge about the human, technical, organizational, and environmental factors that determine the safety of the system as a whole. In most important respects, an informed culture *is* a safety culture.[117] [Emphasis in the original.]

The Metrorail ATC system was designed to prevent collisions by constantly monitoring train locations and slowing or stopping trains as necessary to maintain adequate train separation. Even when trains are operated in manual mode, WMATA expects the ATC system to override operator input if necessary to prevent collisions.

---

[116] *Managing the Risks of Organizational Accidents*, pp. 293–306.

[117] *Managing the Risks of Organizational Accidents*, p. 195.

Keeping the risk of Metrorail injuries and accidents at or near zero requires that WMATA constantly monitor its operations and equipment, disseminate safety-critical information to all affected areas of the organization, and take immediate action to address potential defects. Actively monitoring all safety-critical aspects of an organization for problems is part of maintaining an informed safety culture. However, information gathered during this accident investigation indicates that before the Fort Totten accident, WMATA did not act aggressively to identify and remedy recurring defects in its ATC system. WMATA also did not take operational measures to mitigate the risk of collision until the defects could be corrected.

In this accident, failures to use the loss-of-shunt tool or the enhanced track circuit verification test procedures demonstrate failures to communicate safety-critical information within affected departments of WMATA. The circumstances of this accident exemplify the concerns repeatedly expressed by the NTSB, the FTA, and TOC about the need for coordinated communication of safety-critical functions within WMATA.

Three of the FTA's 10 recommendations issued to WMATA in its March 2010 audit report address safety department deficiencies, including the following: (1) ensure that safety department staff has access to all operations and maintenance information so that potential safety risks can be identified, (2) require that safety-related information be made available to all departments, and (3) develop and implement a process to ensure that the chief safety officer can communicate safety priorities to the general manager in a consistent and timely manner.

The best way to assess the health of safety-critical systems is through active monitoring and evaluation of operations and equipment in search of "leading indicators" of system problems. Examples of leading safety indicators include recorded operational data, the results of inspections, safety audits, and employee reports of safety concerns and near-miss events. The failure of WMATA to measure and address leading indicators of defects in its automatic train detection system suggests that the agency did not fully appreciate the risks represented by aberrations in the ATC system.

Reporting Culture. An informed culture starts with encouraging individuals throughout the organization to report safety-related information and concerns. Safety information is often gathered from accidents and incidents that result in measurable negative outcomes, but safety information can also be gathered from reports of errors, near-misses, and safety concerns that might otherwise go unnoticed. No organization can anticipate all safety problems, but the advantage of actively investigating nonaccident safety lapses is that it may allow an organization to identify and address a system's weaknesses before an accident points them out.[118] The NTSB found examples of a deficient reporting culture within WMATA.

A WMATA ATC engineer who was investigating the June 7, 2005, misrouting of trains at the Rosslyn station, overheard someone stating that the train operators had to apply emergency brakes to avoid colliding in the tunnel between Rosslyn and Foggy Bottom. This piece of

---

[118] R. Flin, "Safety Condition Monitoring: Lessons from 'Man-Made Disasters,'" *Journal of Contingencies and Crisis Management*, vol. 6 (1998), pp. 88–92.

information led the engineer to seek more information on the misrouting and the near-collisions and to contact other engineers to further investigate the incident. However, this information had not been reported, and the engineer learned of it only by chance.

WMATA was required by TOC, under 49 CFR 659.31, to have a process for identifying and resolving hazards. WMATA has several possible sources of information with which to identify potential hazards, including the results of audits and inspections as well as the data recorded in newer railcars and the AIM system used by the OCC. For example, the loss-of-shunt tool uses recorded AIM data to identify potential track circuit malfunctions.

Other modes of transportation have established safety programs for collecting and analyzing recorded operations data and collecting reports of safety concerns and near-misses from frontline personnel, such as vehicle operators and maintenance technicians. In commercial aviation, for example, many airline operators use data from recorders on board their aircraft to monitor trends in operations and identify possible safety concerns. The recorded operational data provide objective safety information that is not otherwise obtainable. The value of operational data analysis programs is the possible early identification of some types of adverse safety trends that, if uncorrected, could lead to accidents.[119]

Similarly, non-punitive self-reporting programs—such as the Federal Aviation Administration's Aviation Safety Action Program[120] and Air Traffic Safety Action Program[121] and the National Aeronautics and Space Administration's Aviation Safety Reporting System[122]—allow individuals to report safety issues without fear that the reports will be used to take disciplinary or enforcement action against them.

The FRA is currently conducting pilot tests of the Confidential Close Call Reporting System (C³RS).[123] The C³RS is a voluntary, confidential program of the FRA, the Bureau of Transportation Statistics (BTS), the DOT Volpe Center, railroad carriers, carrier employees, and labor organizations. Operators implement the reporting system, employees make reports, labor organizations represent employees, the FRA sponsors and oversees the program, the BTS and the Volpe Center act as independent third-party managers, and a peer review team of various stakeholder representatives oversees corrective actions. The C³RS includes several qualities that have been considered critical to the success of other safety reporting systems, including the following:

---

[119] See Federal Aviation Administration Advisory Circular AC 120-82, *Flight Operations Quality Assurance*: <http://www.airweb.faa.gov/Regulatory_and_Guidance_Library/rgAdvisoryCircular.nsf/0/40C02FC39C1577B6862 56E8A005AFB0A >.

[120] See Federal Aviation Administration Advisory Circular AC 120-66B, *Aviation Safety Action Program* (ASAP): <http://www.airweb.faa.gov/Regulatory_and_Guidance_Library/rgAdvisoryCircular.nsf/0/61C319D7A04 907A886256C7900648358 >.

[121] See Federal Aviation Administration Air Traffic Organization Policy Notice N JO 7210.741, *Air Traffic Safety Action Program* (ATSAP): <http://www.faa.gov/documentLibrary/media/Notice/N7210.741.pdf >.

[122] A detailed description is available on the Aviation Safety Reporting System website at <http://asrs.arc.nasa.gov/ >.

[123] Three C³RS demonstration sites are currently in operation, with a fourth scheduled to begin in fall 2010.

- The system is designed to capture close calls, safety concerns, and suggestions from all employees.

- The reporting process is voluntary and designed to maintain reporter confidentiality.

- The system provides the reporter protection from discipline and enforcement action, except in the case of intentional misconduct.

- The system is managed by an independent third-party—in this case, the BTS and the DOT Volpe Center.

- The system includes a mechanism to distribute reports (with identification removed) on safety trends and corrective actions to all participating organizations.

- The system tracks carrier reports on corrective actions to measure system impact on safety.

- The system evaluates and identifies ways to improve reporting system effectiveness.

Regular reviews of recorded data and non-punitive safety reports from these programs have identified safety issues and trends that would not have been readily identified through traditional oversight programs. The NTSB concludes that the safety of rail transit operations would be improved by periodic transit agency review of recorded operational data and non-punitive safety reports, which have been demonstrated to be effective tools for identifying safety problems in other modes of transportation. Therefore, the NTSB recommends that WMATA require that its safety department; representatives of the operations, maintenance, and engineering departments; and representatives of labor organizations regularly review recorded operational data from Metrorail train onboard recorders and the AIM system to identify safety issues and trends and share the results across all divisions of WMATA. The NTSB also recommends that WMATA develop and implement a non-punitive safety reporting program to collect reports from employees in all divisions within WMATA, and ensure that the safety department; representatives of the operations, maintenance, and engineering departments; and representatives of labor organizations regularly review these reports and share the results of those reviews across all divisions of WMATA.

The NTSB further recommends that the FTA facilitate the development of non-punitive safety reporting programs at all transit agencies to collect reports from employees in all divisions within their agencies and to have their safety departments; representatives of their operations, maintenance, and engineering departments; and representatives of labor organizations regularly review these reports and share the results of those reviews across all divisions of their agencies.

Just Culture. Individual behaviors and attitudes toward safety reporting are also influenced by the anticipated response from coworkers and leadership. The comments of the operator of train 214 regarding his decision to operate his train in manual mode are indicative of distrust between WMATA management and its employees. The operator told investigators that he switched from automatic to manual mode when entering the stations because he did not want to rely on the automated system to position the train properly along the platform. WMATA apparently treated improper train positioning in stations as a personnel problem[124] rather than a system problem. Although the train operating mode was routinely displayed in the OCC and recorded by the AIM system, operators choosing to operate in manual mode were never identified as an indication of a system safety concern held by frontline employees.[125] Ideally, safety concerns should be brought to the attention of the safety department and reviewed by a team with expertise from the various agency departments, such as rail operations, track and systems maintenance, and engineering services, for resolution.

Disciplinary practices perceived as unfair can motivate individuals to hide safety-related information or adopt behaviors to avoid blame. In this case, the train 214 operator not only chose to deviate from the policy initially, but he also continued to operate his train in manual mode after being counseled, suggesting that his perceived safety concerns and the threat of discipline for stopping at the wrong position outweighed the threat of discipline for violating the policy regarding operating mode. WMATA's inconsistent enforcement of organizational policies and safety directives is symptomatic of a lack of *just culture* within the agency with regard to safety oversight.

Learning Culture and Shared Concern for Hazards. In order to realize safety improvements, an organization must be capable of drawing the right conclusions from its safety information and must be willing to enact change when needed.

The near-collisions at the Rosslyn station in 2005 provided evidence that the assumed fail-safe design of the ATC system could be compromised and that a catastrophic accident could result. The Rosslyn incident was investigated at the time, and as a result of that investigation, WMATA developed an enhanced track circuit verification test that was intended to identify track circuits with the potential to lose train detection. Also, following a detailed engineering analysis, WMATA developed the loss-of-shunt tool to better monitor track circuit performance. However, the enhanced track circuit verification test was never institutionalized within Metrorail and the loss-of-shunt tool eventually fell into disuse, indicating that WMATA either did not recognize the severity of the risk posed by the hazard identified at Rosslyn or did not communicate that hazard to all departments of the agency. A hazard identification and resolution process[126] was in place at WMATA, as prescribed in its system safety program plan. The results of that hazard assessment should have been distributed to all affected departments of the agency, and the procedures for addressing the identified risk should have been integrated into the training and guidance materials for all affected personnel.

---

[124] See discussion of person-versus-organizational approach to safety in the following section.

[125] The NTSB notes that WMATA has been operating exclusively in manual mode since the accident.

[126] The Hazard Identification and Resolution Matrix process, outlined in Section 6 of the WMATA system safety program plan, is a process for assessing hazard probability and severity of identified safety concerns intended to address TOC's program standards and procedures, which are in turn based on requirements of 49 CFR 659.31. The Hazard Identification and Resolution Matrix is based on the U.S. Department of Defense hazardous risk identification and assessment process specifications of MIL-STD-882 Standard Practice for System Safety <http://safetycenter.navy.mil/instructions/osh/milstd882d.pdf>.

The NTSB concludes that WMATA failed to recognize that the near-collisions at Rosslyn in 2005 represented an unacceptable hazard that had not been considered in the fail-safe design of the ATC system, and WMATA failed to communicate that hazard to the affected divisions in the organization for resolution.

In addition to the problem of communicating safety-critical track circuit information identified by NTSB investigators, the FTA found in its March 2010 audit report of WMATA that WMATA did not have a process that ensures the timely identification and analysis of hazards and that WMATA managers were reactive rather than proactive in assessing and addressing the agency's most serious safety hazards.

The FTA audit report also cited a lack of effective interdepartmental coordination within WMATA with regard to identifying and managing maintenance-related safety hazards. Further, the audit report noted that WMATA lacked a formal process for identifying and managing the likely safety impacts of budgetary decisions that affected equipment maintenance.

The NTSB concludes that, based on the results of this investigation and the FTA's recent safety audit, WMATA was not adequately assessing the severity of hazardous risk associated with identified anomalies in its ATC system. Therefore, the NTSB recommends that WMATA review the Hazard Identification and Resolution Matrix process in its system safety program plan to ensure that safety-critical systems such as the ATC system and its subsystem components are assigned appropriate levels of risk in light of the issues identified in this accident.

WMATA Safety Structure

WMATA's demonstrated deficiencies with regard to identifying safety concerns, distributing safety-critical information across the various affected divisions of the organization, and enacting effective safety policies are symptomatic of a general lack of importance assigned to safety management functions across the organization. During the 5 years before the Fort Totten accident, the chief safety officer had reported variously to WMATA's auditor general, its general manager, its assistant general manager for safety and security, and, at the time of the accident, to the chief administrative officer.

As early as 1996, in its investigation of a Metrorail train collision at the Shady Grove station,[127] the NTSB noted that WMATA employees reported a perceived lack of communication and a sense of information isolation within the organization. As a result, a WMATA safety review committee recommended that WMATA change its organizational structure to have the safety department report directly to the WMATA general manager. Although this internal recommendation was subsequently adopted and implemented, WMATA, after the collision at the Woodley Park station in 2004,[128] restructured its organization and again

---

[127] NTSB/RAR-96/04.

[128] NTSB/RAR-06/01.

removed the direct reporting relationship between the safety department and the general manager. The NTSB expressed its concern about the restructuring in its report on the Woodley Park accident.

TOC also repeatedly expressed concern to WMATA for several years prior to the accident regarding the safety department's position within the organization. As recently as October 2008, TOC sent a letter to the WMATA general manager reiterating its position that there should be a direct reporting relationship between the safety department and the general manager to enable the general manager to adequately support his responsibilities under WMATA's system safety program plan.

Finally, FTA auditors identified a lack of resources dedicated to the safety department within WMATA, a lack of stability within the safety department, and a general lack of attention from senior management.

The current chief safety officer reports directly to the WMATA general manager. However, based on the results of this investigation, testimony during the NTSB public hearing on this accident, and the FTA's audit findings, the NTSB concludes that before the accident, the position of chief safety officer lacked the necessary resources and authority within the organizational structure of WMATA to adequately identify and address system safety issues, ensure the distribution of safety-critical information throughout the organization, or manage the system safety program plan as required by 49 CFR Part 659.

In addition to the specific problems associated with its safety department, WMATA did not vigorously apply the lessons learned from previous Metrorail accidents and incidents, and it did not take effective action to address the many indications of track circuit equipment malfunctions that were evident before the Fort Totten accident. The NTSB concludes that shortcomings in WMATA's internal communications, in its recognition of hazards, its assessment of risk from those hazards, and its implementation of corrective actions are all evidence of an ineffective safety culture within the organization. Further, WMATA did not significantly improve its approach to safety despite various influences such as NTSB accident investigation findings, internal safety committee recommendations, FTA audit findings, and TOC letters. Therefore, the NTSB concludes that previous attempts at non-regulatory oversight failed to compel WMATA to maintain the organizational structure necessary to ensure effective identification and communication of safety-critical information throughout its Metrorail operations.

Oversight of Rail Transit Agencies

The DOT comprises several operating administrations, such as the FRA, that have the authority to promulgate and enforce transportation safety regulations. The FRA governs the operation of standard gage railroads that are part of the general railroad system of transportation, such as freight, intercity passenger, and commuter railroads. Full-time FRA safety inspectors monitor compliance with federally mandated minimum safety standards relating to hazardous materials, motive power and equipment, operating practices, track and signals, and train control. The FRA also collects accident and incident data from the railroads, which it uses to identify trends in railroad safety in general or performance deficiencies of a specific railroad.

Rail transit systems, such as WMATA Metrorail, are not subject to FRA regulation and oversight. These systems fall under the purview of the FTA, whose mission is not to provide regulatory oversight but to provide public transportation agencies with financial, technical, and planning assistance. Although Congress has provided the FTA with regulatory authority with regard to drug and alcohol testing and state safety oversight of rail fixed guideway systems, it has not provided the agency with the authority to directly enforce even those limited regulations.

The NTSB has issued several recommendations to the FTA and its predecessor agencies addressing the need for the FTA to promulgate regulations and to establish mandatory safety guidelines and requirements for recipients of FTA funding. It has been the longstanding position of the FTA that it does not have the legal authority to promulgate regulations or to require an entity that receives funding through the FTA to comply with FTA guidelines and recommended best practices as a condition of federal financial assistance. The extent of the FTA's efforts to this point has been to encourage recipients to adhere to industry best practices and recommendations made by the NTSB.

The FTA's state safety oversight regulation assigns the responsibility for safety oversight to each state. The states carry out that responsibility through a designated oversight agency. The FTA does not, and cannot, provide the oversight agency with the authority to promulgate and enforce safety regulations or standards. Therefore, except for oversight agencies in states such as California and Massachusetts, which have provided their oversight agencies with regulatory and enforcement authority, a state oversight agency is powerless to compel a rail transit agency to comply with its system safety program plan or any other FTA requirement. An oversight agency's lack of authority to establish and enforce safety standards creates a situation in which a rail transit agency can have ineffective and unsatisfactory internal standards leading to failures of safety-critical operations and procedures.

State safety oversight agencies do have the authority to conduct their own accident investigations, but because of staffing limitations or a lack of expertise, this task is often delegated to the rail transit agency itself. If the oversight agency does not agree with the findings of the transit agency's investigation, its only alternatives are to conduct its own investigation or to negotiate with the transit agency until a resolution is reached. The latter leads to situations, as is the case with WMATA Metrorail, in which large numbers of CAPs remain open and unresolved.

The FTA conducts regular audits of each oversight agency to evaluate its compliance with requirements of the state safety oversight regulation. Of the 250 findings that the FTA has made to state oversight agencies since the state safety oversight regulation was revised in May 2006, 55 findings of noncompliance remain open. The FTA effectively can take no action to compel the oversight agency to comply with the actions identified in a CAP. In such cases, the regulation does allow the FTA to withhold up to 5 percent of the funds designated for the state or affected urbanized area, but because these funds are withheld from a state or area and not from the transit agency itself, this option is ineffective in compelling a rail transit agency to comply with the oversight agency's requirements. The NTSB therefore concludes that the structure of the FTA's oversight process leads to inconsistent practices, inadequate standards, and marginal effectiveness with respect to the state safety oversight of rail transit systems in the United States.

Proposed legislation prepared by the DOT in the draft Public Transportation Safety Program Act of 2009, if implemented, would provide the DOT, and therefore the FTA, with the broad authority necessary to address the safety issues identified by the NTSB in its numerous investigations of rail transit accidents. The proposed legislation requires the DOT secretary to establish and implement a public transportation safety program to improve the safety of, and reduce accidents involving, rail fixed guideway transportation systems. Specifically, the secretary would be empowered to prescribe regulations and issue orders for every aspect of rail public transportation systems to ensure the safe operation of such systems. The legislation also requires regulations to establish a safety certification program for individuals involved in safety oversight of rail transit operations. It further allows states to implement more stringent requirements to address local issues so long as those requirements are not inconsistent with federal requirements. The draft legislation also provides authority to the secretary to conduct inspections, investigations, audits, examinations, and testing of a public transportation system's equipment, facilities, rolling stock, operations, and persons engaged in the business.

Although the broad authority proposed in the legislation may be adequate to allow the FTA to address the safety issues raised by the NTSB in its previous accident investigations, the NTSB believes that transit safety will be enhanced if the FTA is given specific authority in a number of areas critical to rail transit safety that have been individually addressed in previous NTSB safety recommendations. Those areas are discussed below.

Crashworthiness

Currently, the FTA has no requirements that address structural crashworthiness provisions for passenger cars operating in transit service. The NTSB believes such minimum crashworthiness standards are necessary to prevent the telescoping of transit railcars in collisions. The NTSB believes that the FTA should be able to establish, develop, and require such standards and to set a reasonable timetable for the mandatory removal from service of older equipment that cannot be modified to meet the new standards. The NTSB's investigation of a 2004 WMATA rail transit accident[129] identified these issues and resulted in the NTSB issuing the following recommendation to the FTA on April 19, 2006:

> Develop minimum crashworthiness standards to prevent the telescoping of transit railcars in collisions and establish a timetable for removing equipment that cannot be modified to meet the new standards. (R-06-6)

---

[129] NTSB/RAR-06/01.

The NTSB added this recommendation to its Most Wanted List of Transportation Safety Improvements in February 2010. This recommendation is currently classified "Open—Acceptable Response."

On June 2, 2010, the FTA responded to Safety Recommendation R-06-6 by stating that while the FTA awaits congressional authority to require crashworthiness standards, it plans to revise 49 CFR Part 659 to address Safety Recommendation R-06-6, in part, by adding a new vehicle safety section to the required system safety program plan elements. Financial support provided to APTA to assist the American Society of Mechanical Engineers has resulted in the issuance of two standards: RT-1 *2009 Safety Standard for Structural Requirements for Light Rail Vehicles* and RT-2 *2008 Safety Standard for Structural Requirements for Heavy Rail Transit Vehicles* that define requirements for the incorporation of passive safety design concepts related to the performance of the carbody of rail transit vehicles in collisions to enhance passenger safety and to limit and control damage.

Safe and Rapid Emergency Responder Entry and Passenger Evacuation

Rail transit cars are not currently required to be equipped with means for safe and rapid emergency responder entry and passenger evacuation. A rapid means of transit railcar ingress and egress can be instrumental in reducing the risks to passengers in the event of a catastrophic accident. The NTSB believes that the FTA should be empowered to develop transit railcar design standards to provide adequate means for safe and rapid emergency responder entry to and passenger evacuation of transit railcars.

In response to the investigation of the Woodley Park accident, the NTSB made a recommendation to the FTA on safe emergency entry to and egress from transit railcars:

> Develop transit railcar design standards to provide adequate means for safe and rapid emergency responder entry and passenger evacuation. (R-06-5)

The NTSB added this recommendation to its Most Wanted List in February 2010. This recommendation is currently classified "Open—Acceptable Response."

On June 2, 2010, FTA responded to Safety Recommendation R-06-5 stating that it needs Congress to grant it the regulatory authority to require emergency ingress and passenger egress standards for rail transit vehicles. In the interim, the FTA has provided additional financial support to APTA to develop voluntary ingress/egress standards for rail transit vehicles including emergency vehicle exits, signs and lighting, low-level exit path markings, and operator protection features, which are expected to be completed in September 2010.

Event Data Recorders

The FTA does not, and currently cannot, require that rail transit cars be equipped with data recorders. Such recorders are often the only means of determining the events, operating conditions, and equipment status in place before an accident. The lack of such information makes it difficult for accident investigators to develop appropriate recommendations to prevent similar accidents in the future. Further, the lack of such information makes it difficult for transit agencies to adequately assess their training and maintenance programs or to evaluate the effectiveness of their operating rules.

Fatigue Management

The FTA does not have hours-of-service regulations for transit vehicle operators. Instead, the agency has delegated the responsibility for fatigue management to the designated state safety oversight agencies to be carried out through the respective system safety program plans. But the regulations describing the general requirements for, and the prescribed contents of, system safety program plans (49 CFR 659.17 and 659.19, respectively) do not contain any requirements or program plan elements that address hours-of-service limits or any other aspect of managing fatigue in the rail transit industry. After the Woodley Park station accident, in which the operator had only 9 hours off between shifts, the NTSB made the following recommendation to the FTA on April 19, 2006:

> Require transit agencies, through the system safety and hazard management process if necessary, to ensure that the time off between daily tours of duty, including regular and overtime assignments, allows train operators to obtain at least 8 hours of uninterrupted sleep. (R-06-3)

The NTSB classified this recommendation "Open—Acceptable Response" on September 23, 2008.

Safety Oversight

The NTSB has long recognized the need to improve the FTA's oversight of rail transit operators and of state oversight agencies. As a result of the safety oversight issues raised in its investigation of the July 11, 2006, derailment of a CTA train in Chicago, Illinois,[130] the NTSB recommended that the FTA develop and implement an action plan, including provisions for technical and financial resources as necessary, to enhance the effectiveness of state safety

---

[130] *Derailment of Chicago Transit Authority Train Number 220 Between Clark/Lake and Grand/Milwaukee Stations, Chicago, Illinois, July 11, 2006*, Railroad Accident Report NTSB/RAR-07/02 (Washington, DC: National Transportation Safety Board, 2007).

oversight programs to identify safety deficiencies and to ensure that those deficiencies are corrected.[131]

These recommendations are in addition to the numerous recommendations the NTSB has made to individual rail transit systems and transit oversight agencies over the years. In almost every case, the lack of adequate federal safety authority has hindered the development of effective federal safety oversight. The NTSB believes that the DOT should ensure that the minimum safety requirements it establishes address the safety issues identified in previous NTSB recommendations, including transit railcar crashworthiness, event recorders, emergency egress/ingress, fatigue, the ability of state safety oversight programs to identify and correct safety deficiencies, and the adequacy of state safety oversight technical and financial resources. The NTSB therefore recommends that the DOT continue to seek the authority to provide safety oversight of rail fixed guideway transportation systems, including the ability to promulgate and enforce safety regulations and minimum requirements governing operations, track and equipment, and signal and train control systems.

State Safety Oversight of WMATA

The designated agency responsible for state oversight of WMATA is TOC. As of early 2010, TOC had identified 48 CAPs that were still classified as open from previous TOC safety audits of WMATA, some of them dating from 2004.

Before the Fort Totten accident, TOC personnel were not permitted on WMATA property to perform field oversight responsibilities without the permission of WMATA. Although this issue has been resolved, TOC's inability to enter the Metrorail system to conduct unannounced audits or inspections significantly diminished its ability to provide the proper safety oversight of Metrorail operations.

The organizational structure and staffing of TOC has the potential for a conflict of interest to develop as it provides its safety oversight function. Because TOC members are employees of the agencies that select them, there exists the potential that their agencies can exercise a level of influence with respect to the decisions and the manner in which TOC provides safety oversight of the Metrorail system. An independent oversight agency would provide a structure that would preclude influence by any of the current parties to the TOC's MOU.

During the FTA's 2007 audit of TOC, the audit team developed 12 findings, 8 of which were for noncompliance. Two of the noncompliance findings were that (1) WMATA had not conducted internal safety audits according to the schedule specified in its system safety program plan and (2) WMATA CAPs were not being reviewed and approved according to the time frame required by TOC program procedures. These were findings that had been identified during the FTA's 2005 audit of TOC and that were carried forward in the 2007 audit report.

---

[131] Safety Recommendations R-07-9 and -10.

The FTA's audit of TOC in 2009 again found shortcomings with the way TOC and WMATA handled issues related to safety. The 2009 FTA findings and recommendations for TOC and WMATA (listed in appendix C of this report) focused on a number of general safety issues noted with both agencies.

For TOC, the FTA's findings addressed, among other issues, (1) providing the resources, financial and personnel, necessary for TOC to carry out its responsibilities and ensuring that TOC members possess the technical and professional skill necessary for the job; (2) improving coordination and communication between WMATA and TOC; (3) resolving previously identified safety issues as well as open CAPs; (4) improving the safety audit process; and (5) ensuring that WMATA has an effective system safety program plan and hazard management program. The NTSB concludes that the results of this investigation, as well as the FTA's audit of TOC and WMATA, determined that TOC has been ineffective in providing proper safety oversight of and lacks the necessary authority to properly oversee the WMATA Metrorail system.

For WMATA, the FTA's recommendations addressed, among other issues, (1) providing the resources and expertise necessary for the WMATA safety department, (2) ensuring that the safety department is actively involved in all operations and maintenance decisions and activities, (3) providing the chief safety officer with direct access to the WMATA general manager, (4) performing a systemwide hazard analysis that involves all WMATA departments, and (5) implementing and providing employee training in new rules to increase worker safety along the WMATA right-of-way.

The NTSB concludes that the results of this investigation and the findings and recommendations contained in the FTA's March 4, 2010, Final Audit Report of its 2009 safety audit of TOC and WMATA, if implemented, will enhance WMATA Metrorail passenger and employee safety. The NTSB therefore recommends that WMATA work with TOC to satisfactorily address the recommendations contained in the FTA's March 4, 2010, final report of its audit of TOC and WMATA. The NTSB further recommends that TOC work with WMATA to satisfactorily address the recommendations contained in the FTA's March 4, 2010, final report of its audit of TOC and WMATA.

Federal Provisions for Transit Employee Toxicological Testing

After the accident, WMATA did not obtain toxicological specimens from the fatally injured operator of train 112. Such a collection was not required by FTA regulation. The FTA requires[132] that

> As soon as practicable following an accident involving the loss of a human life, an employer shall conduct drug and alcohol tests on each surviving covered employee operating the mass transit vehicle at the time of the accident.

---

[132] Title 49 CFR 655.44(a)(1)(i).

The train 112 operator did not survive the accident and thus was not covered by this requirement. U.S. DOT regulations state that a transit agency "must not collect, by catheterization or other means, urine from an unconscious employee to conduct a drug test under this part."[133] This DOT regulation does not address fatally injured employees.

Although the NTSB was able to obtain specimens from the deceased operator under its own authority, it is concerned that specimens cannot be obtained by WMATA or other transit agencies for their transit employees who are fatally injured while on duty. The NTSB notes that, in contrast to FTA regulations, FRA regulations require that drug testing specimens be obtained from a fatally injured railroad employee.[134]

At the time of this accident, federal regulations did not permit transit agencies to collect toxicological specimens from employees killed or rendered unconscious by on-duty accidents. The NTSB concludes that the FTA's lack of toxicological specimen authority prevents transit agencies from collecting pertinent information for determining the circumstances of transit accidents. Therefore, the NTSB recommends that the FTA seek authority similar to FRA regulations (Title 49 CFR 219.207) to require that transit agencies obtain toxicological specimens from covered transit employees and contractors who are fatally injured as a result of an on-duty accident.

Crashworthiness of Metrorail Passenger Cars

The NTSB investigated three previous WMATA Metrorail accidents that raised issues related to the crashworthiness of Metrorail passenger cars.[135] The accident that most closely paralleled the Fort Totten accident in terms of physical damage occurred at Metrorail's Woodley Park station in November 2004.[136] In that accident, a train consisting of 1000-series cars rolled backward down a grade and struck a standing train made up of 4000-series cars. The investigation of the Woodley Park accident determined that the rear car of the rolling train struck the front car of the standing train at an estimated speed of 36 mph. As a result of the collision, the 1000-series rear car of the striking train sustained catastrophic telescoping damage that resulted in a loss of about 34 feet of occupant survival space.[137] The 4000-series lead car of the struck train sustained negligible front-end intrusion damage (less than 2 feet) and suffered essentially no loss of occupant survival space.

Investigation of the Fort Totten accident determined that the front car of train 112 struck the rear car of train 214 at an estimated speed of at least 44 mph. This accident also involved a collision between 1000-series cars and newer cars that were built to later and more robust

---

[133] Title 49 CFR 40.61(b)(3).

[134] 49 CFR 219.207.

[135] See (a) NTSB/RAR-82/06, (b) NTSB/RAR-96/04, and (c) NTSB/RAR-06/01.

[136] NTSB/RAR-06/01.

[137] At the time of the Woodley Park accident, the striking train was unoccupied except for the train operator.

crashworthiness standards. Occupant survivability in the 1000-series lead car of train 112 (where all of the fatalities occurred) was almost exclusively determined by where the occupants were located at the time of the collision. For those occupying the section of the railcar that was subject to the telescoping action, including the train operator's compartment, the accident was essentially non-survivable.

As a result of its investigation of the Woodley Park accident, the NTSB issued the following safety recommendation to WMATA:

> Either accelerate retirement of Rohr-built[138] railcars, or if those railcars are not retired but instead rehabilitated, then the Rohr-built passenger railcars should incorporate a retrofit of crashworthiness collision protection that is comparable to the 6000-series railcars. (R-06-2)

WMATA responded in a January 10, 2007, letter that all cars are fitted with anti-climber features to help prevent carbody override (and thus telescoping in a collision). But as this accident showed, the 1000-series cars were not designed to effectively prevent telescoping. Further, WMATA stated that it was constrained by tax advantage leases, which require that WMATA keep the 1000-series cars in service at least until the end of 2014. WMATA also stated that it was not feasible to retrofit the 1000-series cars and that they would remain in service until replacement with the 7000-series cars in 2014. Based on this response, the NTSB classified Safety Recommendation R-06-2 "Closed—Unacceptable Action" on October 5, 2007.

On August 14, 2009, WMATA sent a letter formally requesting that the NTSB reconsider the status of Safety Recommendation R-06-2 because of WMATA's decision (stated in its January 10, 2007, letter) that it did not intend to perform a heavy overhaul of the 1000-series railcars. The NTSB has, on occasion, reclassified a closed safety recommendation when the recipient has acted in a timely manner after closure to complete the recommended action or has indicated a change in its position and intention to complete the action in a timely manner. WMATA's request, however, came almost 2 years after the recommendation was closed. The 1000-series railcars remain in service, and WMATA did not accelerate the retirement of these cars in response to the NTSB's recommendation. Accordingly, Safety Recommendation R-06-2 remains classified "Closed—Unacceptable Action."

WMATA subsequently informed the NTSB that the 7000-series cars, which are slated to replace the 1000-series cars beginning in 2013, will provide a higher degree of carbody end-structure collision protection than previous Metrorail cars. Although the new series of Metrorail passenger cars will bring a higher level of crashworthiness to the Metrorail fleet, initial delivery of the cars, at best, is about 3 years away. In the meantime, 294 1000-series cars will still be in use, and as shown by this accident and other recent accidents, they represent a serious risk to Metrorail users in the event of a collision. The NTSB concludes that the structural design of the 1000-series railcars offers little occupant protection against a catastrophic loss of occupant survival space in a collision, and the continued use of these cars in revenue service constitutes an

---

[138] Rohr built the 1000-series railcars.

unacceptable risk to WMATA Metrorail users. Therefore, the NTSB recommends that WMATA remove all 1000-series railcars as soon as possible and replace them with cars that have crashworthiness collision protection at least comparable to the 6000-series railcars.

After the Fort Totten accident, WMATA began placing 1000-series cars in the middle (belly) of trains with cars of a later design on either side. This "bellying" of the cars was intended to reduce the vulnerability of the cars to catastrophic damage during a collision. The engineering analysis conducted by WMATA after the NTSB's public hearing on this accident showed a limited benefit to the bellying of 1000-series cars in a low speed collision (that is, below about 15 mph). The NTSB has reviewed WMATA's analysis and notes that bellying the 1000-series cars would not be expected to provide appreciable benefit in higher-speed collisions like those occurring at Fort Totten and Woodley Park.

Significant damage was also sustained by bellied 1000-series cars involved in a recent accident that occurred on November 29, 2009, in the West Falls Church yard (which is currently under investigation by the NTSB). In that accident, the striking train was in nonrevenue service, and the operator was positioning the train behind another train in the yard for servicing. The onboard event data recorder indicated that the speed of the striking train at the time of the collision was about 17 mph. Both trains consisted of six cars, with 5000-series cars in the lead, 1000-series cars in the center (in the "belly"), and 3000-series cars in the trailing position. Three of the four 1000-series cars experienced significantly greater damage than the newer series cars as a result of the collision. Two of these cars were on the struck train, and one of these cars was on the striking train. The end structures of these three 1000-series cars were significantly compromised, and one of the 1000-series cars experienced substantial sidewall outward bowing, all of which is consistent with a loss of structural integrity similar to that found in carbody telescoping. The NTSB concludes that WMATA's practice of bellying the 1000-series cars does not provide appreciable crashworthiness benefits and is not an acceptable substitute for removing the cars from service. The NTSB notes, however, that in the event of an accident, there is a benefit to having event recorders on the lead car of the accident train. The bellying of the 1000-series cars moves these cars without recorders from the lead position and places newer cars, which are normally equipped with event recorders, in the lead. Such positioning could provide critical information for determining the cause of an accident.

Onboard Event Recorders on Metrorail Trains

In this accident, striking train 112 consisted of 1000-series Metrorail cars that were not equipped with onboard event recorders. It also did not have any other source of recorded data. Because of the lack of recording devices on the striking train, NTSB investigators had to compile other sources of information from the investigation to arrive at a best estimate of the striking train's speed, braking performance, and position time history. The NTSB concludes that the lack of onboard event recording capability on the striking train prevented a definitive determination of train performance, the status of the onboard systems, and the operator's actions before the collision.

Although the NTSB recognizes the technical challenges to installing onboard recorders in 1000-series cars, the NTSB is concerned about the continued lack of recorded data for any event involving the 1000- and 4000-series cars. The NTSB notes that an operational event recorder in the lead car of a train will capture critical ATC information as well as train operational data. The NTSB therefore recommends that WMATA ensure that the lead married-pair car set of each train is equipped with an operating onboard event recorder.

Although Metrorail car sets other than 1000- and 4000-series are equipped with onboard recorders, these devices have frequently not been operating when needed. Since December 2006, the NTSB has investigated five WMATA accidents involving trains with onboard recorders. In these accident investigations, only 6 of 11 installed onboard recorders (54.5 percent) were found to contain accident data. As with the Fort Totten accident, the NTSB's investigations were hampered by a lack of recorded data. Investigators have had to gather data from other sources before they could reconstruct accident sequences and evaluate the electronic, mechanical, and human performance factors that led to the accidents.

This investigation determined that WMATA does not have a formal process to ensure the reliability of its onboard recorders. As a result, the recorders cannot do the job for which they were designed. Information received from WMATA indicates that from April 2006 to March 2010, WMATA personnel reported 737 VMS failures that would affect the capturing or recording of train data on the onboard recorder. Because WMATA does not have a program to monitor onboard recorder performance so that such defects are immediately found and remedied, the actual number of failures was likely much higher. The NTSB concludes that because WMATA does not have a program to monitor the performance of onboard event recorders or to ensure that they are functioning properly, these devices cannot be relied upon by WMATA to provide data that can be used for accident investigations or for equipment or operations monitoring and maintenance. The NTSB therefore recommends that WMATA develop and implement a program to monitor the performance of onboard event recorders and ensure they are functioning properly.

Metrorail Passenger Car Emergency Egress

In an emergency, passengers can use the end bulkhead doors to exit from one car into another if the side doors cannot be used and the end doors are not damaged. In this accident, the side doors were not usable, and the end doors between the first car of train 112 and the last car of 214 could not be used because of structural damage.

As noted previously in this report, no federal standards address transit car emergency egress. Safety Recommendation R-06-5, made to the FTA and added to the NTSB's Most Wanted List in 2010, recommended that the FTA develop design standards to address passenger and emergency responder entry and evacuation.

The FTA responded that it is sponsoring the development of a rail transit standard entitled "Emergency Features for Rail Transit Cars." The document is being developed by the

APTA Rail Transit Standards Vehicle Inspection and Maintenance Committee. The project will develop a consensus-based standard to recommend emergency features for inclusion on light and heavy rail transit vehicles. Based on this response, the NTSB classified Safety Recommendation R-06-5 "Open—Acceptable Response."

Conclusions

Findings

1. The following were neither causal nor contributory to the accident: weather, training and qualifications of the train operators, fatigue, use of alcohol or illegal drugs by the train operators, track structure and rail integrity, and condition and performance of train mechanical equipment.

2. The operator's decision to operate train 214 (the struck train) in manual mode during the evening rush hour period was in violation of Metrorail rules, but track circuit B2-304 was failing to detect trains, regardless of whether they were operating in manual or automatic mode.

3. Because train 214, which was being operated in manual mode, was traveling at a much slower speed than the authorized speed commands it was receiving, train 214 stopped completely within the faulty B2-304 track circuit when its detection was lost and it received a 0 mph speed command.

4. Because of the design of the Washington Metropolitan Area Transit Authority (WMATA) operations control center information management system and the high number of track circuit failure alarms routinely generated by that system, operations control center controllers could not have been expected to be aware of the impending collision or to warn either train operator.

5. Considering the challenges of the recovery operations, the emergency response was well coordinated and effectively managed.

6. The Metrorail automatic train control system stopped detecting the presence of train 214 (the struck train) in track circuit B2-304, which caused train 214 to stop and also allowed speed commands to be transmitted to train 112 (the striking train) until the collision.

7. Even though the operator of train 112 activated emergency braking before the collision, there was not enough time, once train 214 came into full view, to stop the train and avoid a collision.

8. On the day of the accident, parasitic oscillation in the track circuit modules for track circuit B2-304 was creating a spurious signal that mimicked a valid track circuit signal, thus causing the track circuit to fail to detect the presence of train 214.

9. Spurious signals had been causing the track circuit modules for track circuit B2-304 to erroneously indicate that the track circuit was vacant from the time the track circuit transmitter power was increased after the impedance bond was replaced on June 17, 2009, until the accident 5 days later.

10. Train operators did not report problems with track circuit B2-304 before the accident because reductions in speed commands to maintain train separation, or even momentary losses of all speed commands, were common during train operations.

11. The track circuit modules did not function safely as part of a fail-safe train control system because General Railway Signal Company (GRS)/Alstom Signaling Inc. did not provide a maintenance plan that would detect anomalies in the track circuit signal, such as parasitic oscillation, over the modules' service life and prevent these anomalies from being interpreted as valid track circuit signals.

12. Some of the GRS track circuit modules in use on the WMATA Metrorail system continue to exhibit parasitic oscillation, and the presence of this oscillation presents an unacceptable risk to Metrorail users.

13. As shown by the fact that (1) the GRS modules in the accident track circuit B2-304 consistently exhibited parasitic oscillation in on-scene and laboratory testing regardless of the type of impedance bond or simulated load used, (2) numerous other Metrorail track circuits that used all GRS components were found to have parasitic oscillation similar to the oscillation found at Fort Totten, and (3) numerous other track circuits with components made by different manufacturers showed no evidence of such oscillation, this accident did not result from WMATA's use of Union Switch & Signal impedance bonds with GRS track circuit modules.

14. The change in transmitter power level necessitated by the installation of a Union Switch & Signal impedance bond in track circuit B2-304 was within the design parameters of the equipment and would not have resulted in a failure of train detection in the absence of parasitic oscillation within the GRS track circuit modules.

15. WMATA failed to institutionalize and employ systemwide the enhanced track circuit verification test developed following the 2005 Rosslyn near-collisions, and this test procedure, had it been formally implemented, would have been sufficient to identify track circuits that could fail in the manner of those at Rosslyn and Fort Totten.

16. If proper shunt placements had been used, as required by WMATA's procedures, to verify track circuit B2-304 either immediately after the new impedance bond was installed on June 17, 2009, or when the track circuit was tested the following day, the work crews would have been able to determine that the track circuit was failing to detect trains, and actions could have been taken to resolve the problem and prevent the accident.

17. A technician following the manufacturer-provided GRS track circuit module maintenance procedures would not have detected the spurious signals that caused track circuit B2-304 to fail in an unsafe manner.

18. WMATA Metrorail automatic train control test procedure T163, developed since this accident, will permit technicians to detect the presence of parasitic oscillation like that found in the failed track circuit modules at Fort Totten; however, unless these procedures are carried out on a periodic basis, an unsafe condition may persist for some time before being discovered and corrected.

19. A comprehensive safety analysis of an automatic train control system must consider all foreseeable system failures that may result in a loss of train separation, including failures in train detection caused by track circuit failures.

20. WMATA did not effectively distribute technical bulletins and safety information to its automatic train control technicians nor did it ensure that the information was received, understood, and properly acted upon by those technicians.

21. WMATA failed to recognize that the near-collisions at Rosslyn in 2005 represented an unacceptable hazard that had not been considered in the fail-safe design of the automatic train control system, and WMATA failed to communicate that hazard to the affected divisions in the organization for resolution.

22. The Metrorail maintenance communication line system—a system that was in disrepair and was apparently no longer needed by WMATA—could allow unanticipated signal paths that could degrade the integrity, and thus the safety, of the Metrorail automatic train control system.

23. As revealed by postaccident testing, the cables serving the impedance bonds for track circuit B2-304 did not meet proposed WMATA Metrorail standards for insulation resistance, and although this did not cause or contribute to the accident, such deficiencies, if undetected and uncorrected, could undermine the safety of the Metrorail train control system.

24. The structure of the Federal Transit Administration's oversight process leads to inconsistent practices, inadequate standards, and marginal effectiveness with respect to the state safety oversight of rail transit systems in the United States.

25. The results of this investigation, as well as the Federal Transit Administration's audit of the Tri-State Oversight Committee and WMATA, determined that the Tri-State Oversight Committee has been ineffective in providing proper safety oversight of and lacks the necessary authority to properly oversee the WMATA Metrorail system.

26. The results of this investigation and the findings and recommendations contained in the Federal Transit Administration's March 4, 2010, Final Audit Report of its 2009 safety audit of the Tri-State Oversight Committee and WMATA, if implemented, will enhance WMATA Metrorail passenger and employee safety.

27. The low priority that WMATA Metrorail managers placed on addressing malfunctions in the train control system before the accident likely influenced the inadequate response to such malfunctions by automatic train control technicians, operations control center controllers, and train operators.

28. The steps that WMATA has taken since the Fort Totten accident, such as improving and increasing the use of the loss-of-shunt software tool for identifying track circuit malfunctions, will contribute to improving the safety of the system.

29. The safety of rail transit operations would be improved by periodic transit agency review of recorded operational data and non-punitive safety reports, which have been demonstrated to be effective tools for identifying safety problems in other modes of transportation.

30. Based on the results of this investigation and the Federal Transit Administration's recent safety audit, WMATA was not adequately assessing the severity of hazardous risk associated with identified anomalies in its automatic train control system.

31. The WMATA Board of Directors did not exercise oversight responsibility for the system safety of the WMATA system.

32. Before the accident, the WMATA Board of Directors did not seek adequate information about, nor did it demonstrate adequate oversight to address, the number of open corrective action plans from previous Tri-State Oversight Committee and Federal Transit Administration safety audits of WMATA.

33. Before the accident, the position of chief safety officer lacked the necessary resources and authority within the organizational structure of WMATA to adequately identify and address system safety issues, ensure the distribution of safety-critical information throughout the organization, or manage the system safety program plan as required by Title 49 *Code of Federal Regulations* Part 659.

34. Shortcomings in WMATA's internal communications, in its recognition of hazards, its assessment of risk from those hazards, and its implementation of corrective actions are all evidence of an ineffective safety culture within the organization.

35. Previous attempts at non-regulatory oversight failed to compel WMATA to maintain the organizational structure necessary to ensure effective identification and communication of safety-critical information throughout its Metrorail operations.

36. The FTA's lack of toxicological specimen authority prevents transit agencies from collecting pertinent information for determining the circumstances of transit accidents.

37. The structural design of the 1000-series railcars offers little occupant protection against a catastrophic loss of occupant survival space in a collision, and the continued use of these cars in revenue service constitutes an unacceptable risk to WMATA Metrorail users.

38. WMATA's practice of bellying the 1000-series cars does not provide appreciable crashworthiness benefits and is not an acceptable substitute for removing the cars from service.

39. The lack of onboard event recording capability on the striking train prevented a definitive determination of train performance, the status of the onboard systems, and the operator's actions before the collision.

40. Because WMATA does not have a program to monitor the performance of onboard event recorders or to ensure that they are functioning properly, these devices cannot be relied upon by WMATA to provide data that can be used for accident investigations or for equipment or operations monitoring and maintenance.

Probable Cause

The National Transportation Safety Board determines that the probable cause of the June 22, 2009, collision of Washington Metropolitan Area Transit Authority (WMATA) Metrorail train 112 with the rear of standing train 214 near the Fort Totten station was (1) a failure of the track circuit modules, built by GRS/Alstom Signaling Inc., that caused the automatic train control system to lose detection of train 214 (the struck train) and thus transmit speed commands to train 112 (the striking train) up to the point of impact, and (2) WMATA's failure to ensure that the enhanced track circuit verification test (developed following the 2005 Rosslyn near-collisions) was institutionalized and used systemwide, which would have identified the faulty track circuit before the accident.

Contributing to the accident were (1) WMATA's lack of a safety culture, (2) WMATA's failure to effectively maintain and monitor the performance of its automatic train control system, (3) GRS/Alstom Signaling Inc.'s failure to provide a maintenance plan to detect spurious signals that could cause its track circuit modules to malfunction, (4) ineffective safety oversight by the WMATA Board of Directors, (5) the Tri-State Oversight Committee's ineffective oversight and lack of safety oversight authority, and (6) the Federal Transit Administration's lack of statutory authority to provide federal safety oversight.

Contributing to the severity of passenger injuries and the number of fatalities was WMATA's failure to replace or retrofit the 1000-series railcars after these cars were shown in a previous accident to exhibit poor crashworthiness.

Recommendations

As a result of its investigation of this accident, the National Transportation Safety Board makes the following safety recommendations.

New Recommendations

To the U.S. Department of Transportation:

Continue to seek the authority to provide safety oversight of rail fixed guideway transportation systems, including the ability to promulgate and enforce safety regulations and minimum requirements governing operations, track and equipment, and signal and train control systems. (R-10-3)

To the Federal Transit Administration:

Facilitate the development of non-punitive safety reporting programs at all transit agencies to collect reports from employees in all divisions within their agencies and to have their safety departments; representatives of their operations, maintenance, and engineering departments; and representatives of labor organizations regularly review these reports and share the results of those reviews across all divisions of their agencies. (R-10-4)

Seek authority similar to Federal Railroad Administration regulations (Title 49 *Code of Federal Regulations* 219.207) to require that transit agencies obtain toxicological specimens from covered transit employees and contractors who are fatally injured as a result of an on-duty accident. (R-10-5)

To the Tri-State Oversight Committee:

Work with the Washington Metropolitan Area Transit Authority to satisfactorily address the recommendations contained in the Federal Transit Administration's March 4, 2010, final report of its audit of the Tri-State Oversight Committee and the Washington Metropolitan Area Transit Authority. (R-10-6)

To the Board of Directors, Washington Metropolitan Area Transit Authority:

Elevate the safety oversight role of the Washington Metropolitan Area Transit Authority Board of Directors by (1) developing a policy statement to explicitly and publicly assume the responsibility for continual oversight of system safety, (2) implementing processes to exercise oversight of system safety, including appropriate proactive performance metrics, and (3) evaluating actions taken in response to National Transportation Safety Board and Federal Transit Administration recommendations, as well as the status of open corrective action plans and the results of audits conducted by the Tri-State Oversight Committee. (R-10-7)

To the Washington Metropolitan Area Transit Authority:

Because of the susceptibility to pulse-type parasitic oscillation that can cause a loss of train detection by the Generation 2 General Railway Signal Company audio frequency track circuit modules, establish a program to permanently remove from service all of these modules within the Metrorail system. (R-10-8)

Establish periodic inspection and maintenance procedures to examine all audio frequency track circuit modules within the Metrorail system to identify and remove from service any modules that exhibit pulse-type parasitic oscillation. (R-10-9)

Review the process by which Metrorail technical bulletins and other safety information are provided to employees and revise that process as necessary to ensure that (1) employees have received the information intended for them, (2) employees understand the actions to be taken in response to the information, and (3) employees take the appropriate actions. (R-10-10)

Completely remove the unnecessary Metrorail wayside maintenance communication system to eliminate its potential for interfering with the proper functioning of the train control system. (R-10-11)

Conduct a comprehensive safety analysis of the Metrorail automatic train control system to evaluate all foreseeable failures of this system that could result in a loss of train separation, and work with your train control equipment manufacturers to address in that analysis all potential failure modes that could cause a loss of train detection, including parasitic oscillation, cable faults and placement, and corrugated rail. (R-10-12)

Based on the findings of the safety analysis recommended in R-10-12 incorporate the design, operational, and maintenance controls necessary to address potential failures in the automatic train control system. (R-10-13)

Implement cable insulation resistance testing as part of Metrorail's periodic maintenance program. (R-10-14)

Work with the Tri-State Oversight Committee to satisfactorily address the recommendations contained in the Federal Transit Administration's March 4, 2010, final report of its audit of the Tri-State Oversight Committee and the Washington Metropolitan Area Transit Authority. (R-10-15)

Require that your safety department; representatives of the operations, maintenance, and engineering departments; and representatives of labor organizations regularly review recorded operational data from Metrorail train onboard recorders and the Advanced Information Management system to identify safety issues and trends and share the results across all divisions of your organization. (R-10-16)

Develop and implement a non-punitive safety reporting program to collect reports from employees in all divisions within your organization, and ensure that the safety department; representatives of the operations, maintenance, and engineering departments; and representatives of labor organizations regularly review these reports and share the results of those reviews across all divisions of your organization. (R-10-17)

Review the Hazard Identification and Resolution Matrix process in your system safety program plan to ensure that safety-critical systems such as the automatic train control system and its subsystem components are assigned appropriate levels of risk in light of the issues identified in this accident. (R-10-18)

Develop a formal process by which the general manager and managers responsible for Washington Metropolitan Area Transit Authority operations, maintenance, and engineering will periodically review, in collaboration with the chief safety officer, all safety audits and open corrective action plans, and modify policy, identify and commit resources, and initiate any other action necessary to ensure that the plans are adequately addressed and closed within the required time frame. (R-10-19)

Remove all 1000-series railcars as soon as possible and replace them with cars that have crashworthiness collision protection at least comparable to the 6000-series railcars. (R-10-20)

Ensure that the lead married-pair car set of each train is equipped with an operating onboard event recorder. (R-10-21)

Develop and implement a program to monitor the performance of onboard event recorders and ensure they are functioning properly. (R-10-22)

To Alstom Signaling Inc.:

Develop and implement periodic inspection and maintenance guidelines for use by the Washington Metropolitan Area Transit Authority and other rail transit operators and railroads equipped with General Railway Signal Company audio frequency track circuit modules and assist them in identifying and removing from service all modules that exhibit pulse-type parasitic oscillation in order to ensure the vitality and integrity of the automatic train control system. (R-10-23)

Conduct a comprehensive safety analysis of your audio frequency track circuit modules to evaluate all foreseeable failure modes that could cause a loss of train detection over the service life of the modules, including parasitic oscillation, and work with your customers to address these failure modes. (R-10-24)

To the Massachusetts Bay Transportation Authority, the Southeastern Pennsylvania Transportation Authority, the Greater Cleveland Regional Transit Authority, the Metropolitan Atlanta Regional Transportation Authority, the Los Angeles County Metropolitan Transportation Authority, and the Chicago Transit Authority:

Work with Alstom Signaling Inc. to establish periodic inspection and maintenance procedures to examine all General Railway Signal Company audio frequency track circuit modules to identify and remove from service any modules that exhibit pulse-type parasitic oscillation. (R-10-25)

Previously Issued Recommendations

As a result of this accident investigation, the National Transportation Safety Board previously issued the following safety recommendations:

To the Federal Transit Administration:

Advise all rail transit operators that have train control systems capable of monitoring train movements to determine whether their systems have adequate safety redundancy if losses in train detection occur. If a system is susceptible to single point failures, urge and verify that corrective action is taken to add redundancy by evaluating track occupancy data on a real-time basis to automatically generate alerts and speed restrictions to prevent train collisions. (R-09-7 Urgent) (Currently classified "Open—Acceptable Response.")

Advise all rail transit operators that use audio frequency track circuits in their train control systems that postaccident testing following the June 22, 2009, collision between two rail transit trains near the Fort Totten station in Washington, D.C., identified that a spurious signal generated in a track circuit module transmitter by parasitic oscillation propagated from the transmitter through a metal rack to an adjacent track circuit module receiver, and through a shared power source, thus establishing an unintended signal path. The spurious signal mimicked a valid track circuit signal, bypassed the rails, and was sensed by the module receiver so that the ability of the track circuit to detect the train was lost. (R-09-17 Urgent) (Classified "Closed—Acceptable Action.")

Advise all rail transit operators that use audio frequency track circuits in their train control systems to examine track circuits that may be susceptible to parasitic oscillation and spurious signals capable of exploiting unintended signal paths and eliminate those adverse conditions that could affect the safe performance of their train control systems. This work should be conducted in coordination with their signal and train control equipment manufacturers. (R-09-18 Urgent) (Classified "Closed—Acceptable Action.")

Advise all rail transit operators that use audio frequency track circuits in their train control systems to develop a program to periodically determine that electronic components in their train control systems are performing within design tolerances. (R-09-19) (Currently classified "Open—Acceptable Response.")

To the Federal Railroad Administration:

Advise all railroads that use audio frequency track circuits in their train control systems that postaccident testing following the June 22, 2009, collision between two rail transit trains near the Fort Totten station in Washington, D.C., identified that a spurious signal generated in a track circuit module transmitter by parasitic oscillation propagated from the transmitter through a metal rack to an adjacent track circuit module receiver, and through a shared power source, thus establishing an unintended signal path. The spurious signal mimicked a valid track circuit signal, bypassed the rails, and was sensed by the module receiver so that the ability of the track circuit to detect the train was lost. (R-09-20 Urgent) (Classified "Closed—Acceptable Action."

Require all railroads that use audio frequency track circuits in their train control systems to examine track circuits that may be susceptible to parasitic oscillation and spurious signals capable of exploiting unintended signal paths and eliminate those adverse conditions that could affect the safe performance of their train control systems. This work should be conducted in coordination with their signal and train control equipment manufacturers. (R-09-21 Urgent) (Currently classified "Open—Acceptable Response.")

Require all railroads that use audio frequency track circuits in their train control systems to develop a program to periodically determine that electronic components in their train control systems are performing within design tolerances. (R-09-22) (Currently classified "Open—Acceptable Response.")

To Washington Metropolitan Area Transit Authority:

Take action to enhance the safety redundancy of your train control system by evaluating track occupancy data on a real-time basis in order to detect losses in track occupancy and automatically generate alerts. Alerts should prompt actions that include immediately stopping train movements or implementing appropriate speed restrictions to prevent collisions. (R-09-6 Urgent) (Currently classified "Open—Acceptable Response.")

Develop a program to periodically determine that electronic components in your train control system are performing within design tolerances. (R-09-16) (Currently classified "Open—Initial Response Received.")

Previously Issued Recommendations Reclassified in This Report

To Washington Metropolitan Area Transit Authority:

Examine track circuits within your system that may be susceptible to parasitic oscillation and spurious signals capable of exploiting unintended signal paths, and eliminate those adverse conditions that could affect the safe performance of your train control system. This work should be conducted in coordination with your signal and train control equipment manufacturer(s). (R-09-15 Urgent)

Urgent Safety Recommendation R-09-15, previously classified "Open—Acceptable Response," is reclassified "Closed—Superseded" by Safety Recommendation R-10-8.

To Alstom Signaling Inc.:

Assist the Washington Metropolitan Area Transit Authority, and other rail transit operators and railroads that use your audio frequency track circuit equipment, in examining their train control systems for susceptibility to parasitic oscillations and spurious signals capable of exploiting unintended signal paths, and implementing measures to eliminate those adverse conditions that could affect the safe performance of their train control systems. (R-09-23 Urgent)

Urgent Safety Recommendation R-09-23, previously classified "Open—Acceptable Response," is reclassified "Closed—Superseded" by Safety Recommendations R-10-23 and -25.

BY THE NATIONAL TRANSPORTATION SAFETY BOARD

DEBORAH A.P. HERSMAN
Chairman

ROBERT L. SUMWALT
Member

CHRISTOPHER A. HART
Vice Chairman

EARL F. WEENER
Member

MARK R. ROSEKIND
Member

Adopted: July 27, 2010

Appendix A

Investigation

The National Transportation Safety board (NTSB) was notified of the accident about 5:30 p.m. on June 22, 2009. The investigator-in-charge and other members of the NTSB investigative team were launched from the headquarters office in Washington, D.C., and from field offices in Chicago, Illinois, and Gardena, California. The NTSB's investigation focused on all aspects of the accident, including signal and train control, operations, track, mechanical issues, human performance, survival factors, crashworthiness, event recorders, and safety culture/oversight issues. Member Deborah A.P. Hersman was the Board Member on scene.

Parties to the investigation were the Federal Transit Administration, the Federal Railroad Administration, the Washington Metropolitan Area Transit Authority, the Amalgamated Transit Union, the Tri-State Oversight Committee, the District of Columbia Fire and Emergency Medical Services Department, Alstom Signaling Inc., and Ansaldo STS USA.

Public Hearing

A public hearing on this accident was held at the NTSB Conference Center in Washington, D.C., on February 23–25, 2010. The hearing was chaired by Member Robert L. Sumwalt.

Appendix B

Accident Sequence as Displayed on Controller Screen at Metrorail Operations Control Center

The images below depict the Metrorail Operations Control Center (OCC) screen display during the accident sequence. These images are enlargements of a small portion of a controller's display screen and thus do not represent the actual view available to the OCC controller.

The text below each image provides the time of day and a description of the train movements and the status of track circuits at that time. Main line track is shown as a linked row of colored rectangles, with each rectangle representing a track circuit. (Track circuit identifications have been added to the images; they do not appear on the actual displays.) A rectangle representing an unoccupied block of track (no train present) is gray. An occupied block is red. The presence of a train is indicated by a string of red (occupied) blocks with a red arrow superimposed at one end showing the train number, the operating mode (manual or automatic), and the direction of travel. Wayside signals are depicted as circular icons that indicate red or green depending on the status of the signal.

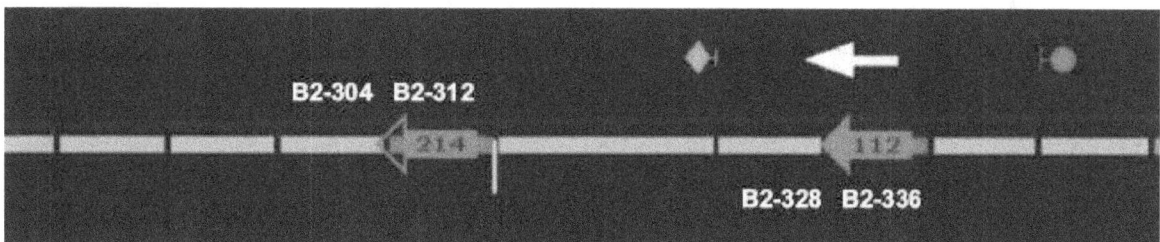

4:56:50 p.m. Train 214 is detected occupying track circuit B2-312, with train 112 several blocks behind on track circuit B2-336. Red track circuit symbols indicate track occupancy. The transparent arrowhead for train 214 indicates that the train is being operated in manual mode. Performance data indicated that the front of train 214 was actually at chain marker 315+00, corresponding to track circuit B2-312. The front of train 112 was actually at chain marker 338+48, corresponding to track circuit B2-336. The solid arrowhead for train 112 indicates that this train is in automatic mode.

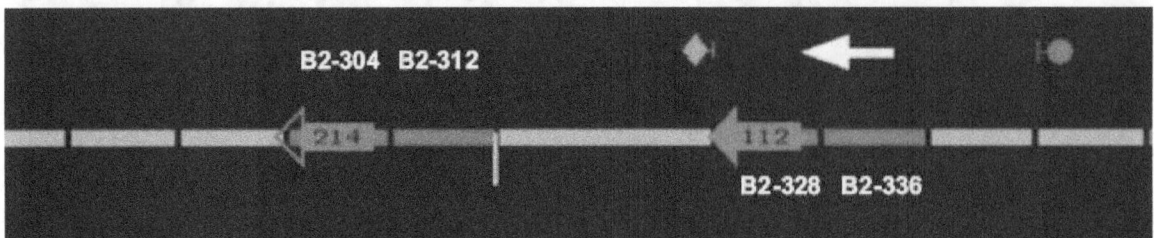

4:57:02 p.m. Both trains have moved forward into the next block in their direction of travel. Track occupancy is being detected on track circuits B2-304 and B2-312 for train 214 and on track circuits B2-328 and B2-336 for train 112. Performance data indicated that the front of train 214 was at chain marker 312+00, corresponding to track circuit B2-312. The front of train 112 was at chain marker 335+70, corresponding to track circuit B2-328.

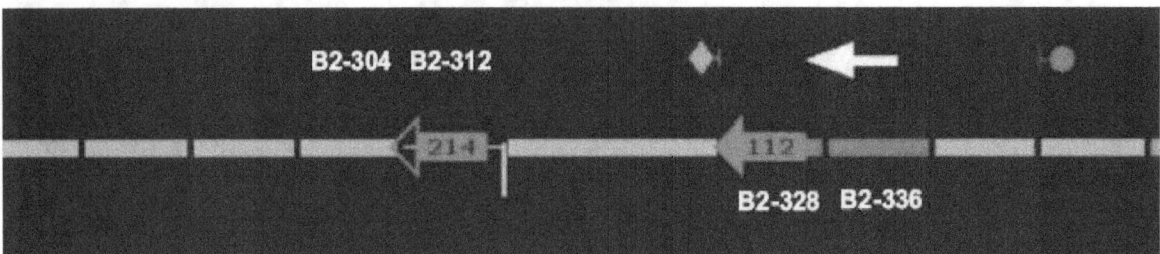

4:57:19 p.m. Train 214 is depicted as occupying a single track circuit (B2-312) that is shown as a non-reporting block (a track circuit that reports as vacant when Advanced Information Management system computer algorithms determine that it should be occupied). Track circuit B2-304 displays as an unoccupied, normally reporting block. Performance data indicated that train 214 was stopped at this time and that the front of train 214 was actually at chain marker 307+00, corresponding to track circuit B2-304. The front of train 112 was at chain marker 335+69, corresponding to track circuit B2-328. Track circuit B2-304 displays as a normally reporting, unoccupied block even though performance data indicated that train 214 was fully within that track circuit. Performance data also indicated that at this time train 112 had begun receiving speed commands of 55 mph.

4:57:38 p.m. Track circuit B2-304 displays as unoccupied even though performance data indicated that the front of train 214 was at chain marker 307+00, corresponding to track circuit B2-304. Track circuit B2-312 is now displaying as an occupied, normally reporting block. The tag for train 214 has been dropped from the display as a result of preprogrammed Advanced Information Management system algorithms designed to eliminate false train indications. The front of train 112 was at chain marker 330+15, corresponding to track circuit B2-328.

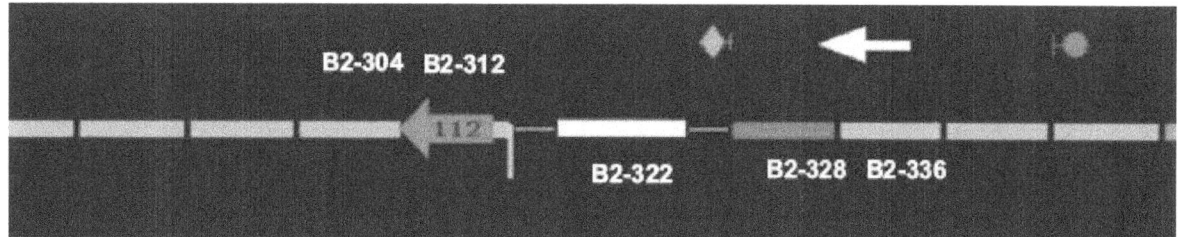

4:57:39 p.m. Train 214 is gone from the display. Train 112 is displayed as occupying a single track circuit (B2-312), which is now reporting as an unoccupied block. At this time, performance data indicated that the front of train 214 was at chain marker 307+00, corresponding to track circuit B2-304. The front of train 112 was at chain marker 329+52, corresponding to track circuit B2-328. Track circuit B2-328 is displayed as an occupied block. The intervening track circuit (B2-322) is displayed as an unoccupied, non-reporting block. Track circuit B2-304 is displayed as unoccupied even though all of train 214 is occupying that track circuit.

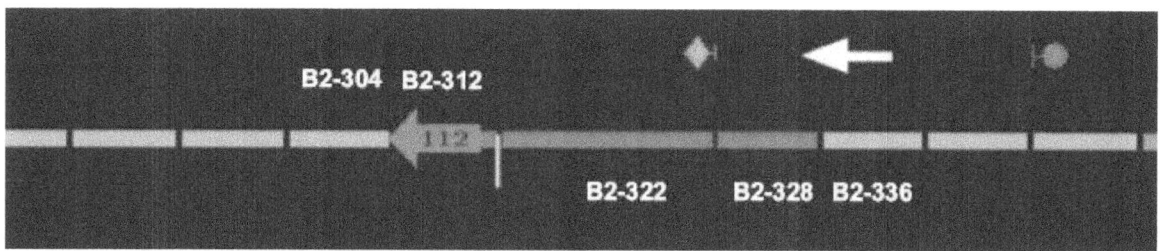

4:57:46 p.m. Train 112 is displayed as occupying three track circuits, all of which are displayed as normally reporting blocks. Performance data indicated that the front of train 214 was actually at chain marker 307+00, corresponding to track circuit B2-304. The front of train 112 was at chain marker 324+64, corresponding to track circuit B2-322.

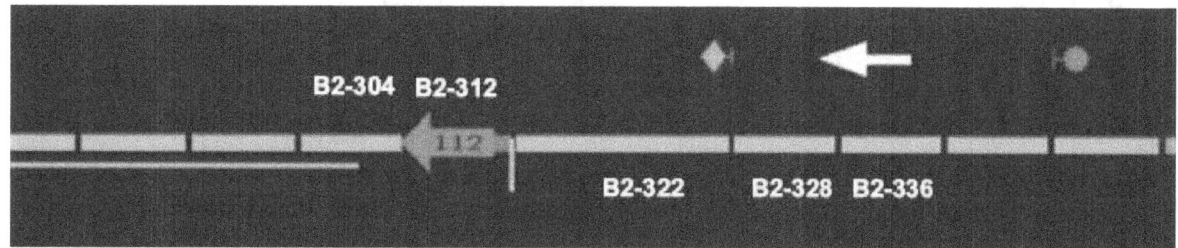

4:58:10 p.m. Train 112 is displayed as occupying a single track circuit (B2-312). All track circuits are now displayed as normally reporting blocks. The green line indicates that third-rail power is down ahead of B2-312. Performance data indicated that the front of train 214 was actually at chain marker 307+00, corresponding to track circuit B2-304. The front of train 112 was at chain marker 311+00, also corresponding to track circuit B2-304.

Appendix C

Findings and Recommendations From Federal Transit Administration 2009 Audit of the Tri-State Oversight Committee and the Washington Metropolitan Area Transit Authority

The Federal Transit Administration (FTA) conducted an on-site audit of the safety program implemented by the Washington Metropolitan Area Transit Authority (WMATA) and overseen by the Tri-State Oversight Committee (TOC) between December 14 and 17, 2009.[139] The findings and recommendations resulting from that audit are as follows:

Findings to the Tri-State Oversight Committee:

1. Assess the level of resources necessary from each jurisdiction (District of Columbia, Maryland and Virginia) to meet TOC's responsibilities. Use the results of this assessment to establish resource commitments from each jurisdiction to TOC for the next three calendar years. Resources should be committed and onboard before the beginning of the next Federal audit cycle.

2. Evaluate the technical and professional skills that TOC representatives need to effectively carry out their oversight duties. To the extent that TOC representatives do not currently possess these skills, ensure training is provided as soon as practicable to each TOC member.

3. Determine the best method to respond quickly and professionally, as WMATA safety situations arise and require coordinated action. Consider whether full-time TOC positions can be vested with decision-making authority to act in specific safety situations with WMATA.

4. Identify and formalize a mechanism to ensure that critical unresolved WMATA safety concerns identified by TOC members are elevated to the highest levels of each TOC jurisdictional agency and WMATA for immediate action.

5. Require WMATA to complete a timely, thorough, and competent review and update of WMATA's Safety Rules and Procedures Manual. This review and update must reflect actual current practices and needed improvements identified by TOC and by FTA in this audit report.

---

[139] *State Safety Oversight Program: Audit of the Tri-State Oversight Committee and the Washington Metropolitan Area Transit Authority, Final Audit Report* (Washington, DC: U.S. Department of Transportation, Federal Transit Administration, 2010).

6. Require WMATA to develop (and TOC to review and approve) an internal WMATA safety audit recovery plan for calendar year 2010 and calendar year 2011. Before WMATA develops this plan, TOC should sponsor a meeting with WMATA's Safety Department, Quality Department, and Executive Leadership Team to explain the internal safety audit program requirements and TOC's expectations regarding WMATA's internal safety audit recovery plan.

7. Require WMATA to develop a recovery plan to complete all open accident investigations following procedures established in TOC's Program Standard, WMATA's System Safety Program Plan and WMATA's Accident Investigation Procedures.

8. Document the Corrective Action Plan Technical Review process in TOC's Program Standard and Procedures and WMATA's System Safety Program Plan.

9. Work with WMATA to ensure that there is a process in place for evaluating Corrective Action Plans (CAP) alternatives that may be necessary as a result of capital and operating program resource limitations.

10. Require WMATA to develop and implement a comprehensive and system-wide hazard management program (as required by [Title] 49 [*Code of Federal Regulations*] CFR Part 659.31).

11. Require WMATA to strictly adhere to the annual certification of compliance with its System Safety Program Plan (as specified in 49 CFR 659.43), including identifying areas where WMATA is not in compliance with its System Safety Program Plan as well as specific actions WMATA is taking to achieve compliance.

Recommendations to the Washington Metropolitan Area Transit Authority:

1. Conduct an assessment to identify the resources and expertise necessary for the Safety Department to carry out the activities specified in WMATA's System Safety Program Plan and Safety Rules and Procedures Manual.

2. Use the results of the assessment to ensure adequate staffing levels and expertise within the Safety Department.

3. Increase the Safety Department's access to operating and maintenance information and reports to ensure that this information is being analyzed for potential impacts on the safety of WMATA.

4. Develop an internal process to require the communication of safety-related information across all WMATA departments, including the impacts of budget reductions and resource constraints on the performance of safety-related maintenance activities and requirements.

5. Define and implement the process for the top Safety Department position to communicate safety priorities to the General Manager in a timely and consistent manner.

6. Identify the technical skills required to perform system-wide hazard analysis (as required in 49 CFR Part 659 and TOC's Program Standard). To the extent that WMATA Safety Department staff does not currently possess the needed skills, provide training as soon as practicable.

7. Update the WMATA System Safety Program Plan (specifically Procedure #2.1/0 and Section 6) to develop a hazard management process that ensures that all WMATA departments participate in an on-going manner.

8. Institute a process to ensure that changes in operating rules are analyzed for safety impacts before system-wide implementation. For example, WMATA engineering bulletins are "field tested" before full implementation.

9. Finalize the right-of-way protection rules, develop training to implement the new rules and ensure all right-of-way employees and contractors receive this training before accessing the right-of-way.

10. Implement the configuration management program described in the WMATA System Safety Program Plan.